Gaell Lindstrom,
My Father

co-authored by Braden Lindstrom

*Painter of Life and Land in Utah and
Beyond: The Art of Gaell Lindstrom*

Gaell Lindstrom, My Father

by Dr. Braden Lindstrom

Foreword by Ardeshir Zahedi

OCCIDENTAL SQUARE PRESS
Seattle, 2019

Gaell Lindstrom, My Father by Braden Lindstrom.

Text copyright the author, 2019. All Images copyright.

Edited by Phil Bevis and Tori Champion,
assisted by Annie Brulé, Helen Pendergast, Judith Feenstra. and Cyra Jane Hobson

Interior design by Cyra Jane Hobson.
Cover design by Phil Bevis.
All rights reserved.

Cover photography:

Paperback ISBN: 978-1-63398-107-2

Occidental Square Books is an imprint of Chatwin Books.

www.ChatwinBooks.com
info@chatwinbooks.com

Table of Contents

Foreword

In the late 1940's, I was an undergraduate student at the College of Agriculture and Applied Sciences, now Utah State University. Courses on comparative art did not appear on our syllabus, but I knew Professor Lindstrom by his reputation. His exhibitions of watercolour were amongst the great events on the campus. Friends and compatriots in the Department of Art also told me about his academic qualities, the versatility of his artistic talents, and above all the gracious manners of this unassuming man. He spent some three decades of his life at USU, and served under President Daryl Chase with whom I had close and friendly association.

Less than a decade later, when I was on my first mission in Washington, D.C. as the Iranian Ambassador to the United States, I invited President Chase to visit the Iranian pavilion at an international fair in Chicago. He was accompanied by his lifelong friend and colleague, Professor Gaell Lindstrom. It was then that I started to discover Lindstrom's true talents as a great painter and photographer. He also impressed me by his learned comments on Iranian contributions to art and culture.

Today, I am happy to see that his son, Braden, himself a distinguished academician, has written this book on his father, an inspiring figure both as an artist and as a man. The work would certainly be a welcome addition to the library of anyone interested in comparative art and in the history of Utah State University, where I was reborn.

—Ardeshir Zahedi

*Former Iranian Ambassador to the United States
and Iran Minister of Affairs*

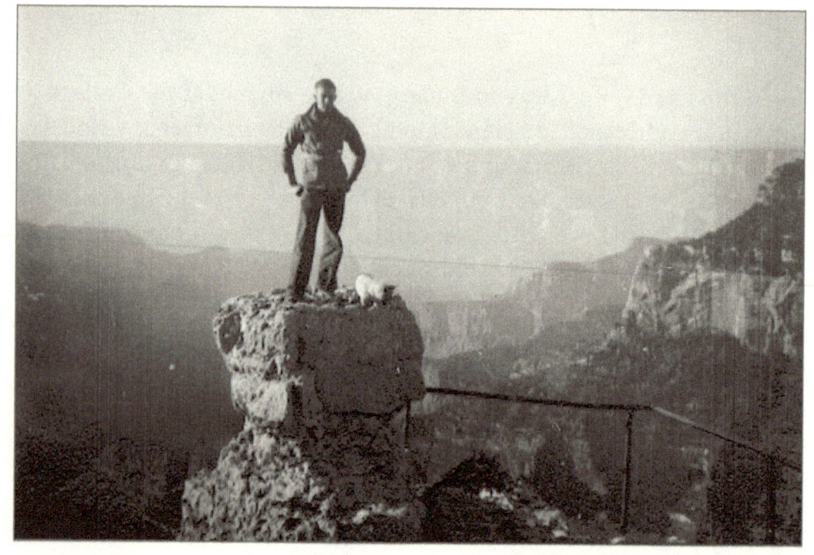

Gale Lindstrom in Arizona, 1937

Preface

Painter. Potter. Photographer. Although his work can be found in private and public collections throughout the United States, Gaell Lindstrom is not well-known outside of his native Utah. Save for two years in Kentucky, Tennessee, and West Virginia as a church missionary, he lived his entire life in the Beehive State teaching art, first at Cedar City Junior High School and then for 27 years in Logan at Utah State University (USU). He won national recognition from the American Watercolor Society, Watercolor U.S.A., and the National Academy of Design, but many of the awards for his work are from state and county contests.

He photographed and painted landscapes of southern Idaho, Panaca, Nevada, Arizona's Oak Creek Canyon, and throughout his beloved Utah including Logan Canyon, Smithsonian Butte, and Zion National Park. In his work he moved freely from landscapes to cities to figures—"the most important thing is not the mountains nor the cityscapes but the people," he said. He was a street artist who, in his own words, "became imbued with lights and darks in any subject matter."

Although he is closely associated with his native state, Lindstrom did not consider himself a regional artist. His paintings depict subjects not only in the American West, but the U.S. East Coast, Mexico, Central America, Asia, Europe, and North Africa, and vary in style, medium, and subject. He wrote: "One ought not to be too pleased with one's work. Nor should one always use the same technique and materials and only change the subject. Creativity is not well served with this approach." He experimented with block printing, evoked the tangled branches of trees by splattering canvases with rubber cement to resist paint, and glued colored tissue paper to other canvases to give his watercolors texture and an element of abstraction.

Lindstrom had a photographic memory and could intelligently converse in depth on a wide range of topics and people from art history to aviation, Bach to Brahms, geology to gastronomy, politics to pool,

John Wesley Powell to Joseph Smith. As a lay church teacher, he once centered a lesson on Smith contemplating Benjamin West's painting *Death on a Pale Horse*. In the last year of his life, the books on his shelves included *The Canterbury Tales, Of Gods and Men: Mexico and the Mexican Indian, Invitation to Venice, Chinese Calligraphy,* and *The Discoverers: A History of Man's Search to Know His World and Himself.* He played the recorder, trumpet, French horn, and piano.

He was a Renaissance man and my father.

I took the title of this book from film director Jean Renoir's biography of his father, Pierre-Auguste Renoir, who died the year Lindstrom was born. Lindstrom knew and admired the work of Pierre, and would be a little embarrassed and believe my title selection pretentious. But like Jean, I greatly admired my father and his work, and, as an aspiring filmmaker, I hoped the title might be a good omen.

—*Braden Lindstrom*

Chapter 1:

The Traveler

I've only been arrested once in my life and it was my father's fault.

In the summer of 2018, while walking down a street near the International Bazaar in Urumqi, China, I spotted an elderly woman wearing a bright orange vest sitting in front of the faux brick wall of a health clinic. I hurried to change the camera lens (I had forgotten my father's advice: put your zoom lens on the camera and leave it there), snapped a few ho-hum photos of her, and was promptly stopped by plainclothes police officers. Urumqi is the capital of China's restless province of Xinjiang, the site of 2009 protests that turned deadly. I tried to keep walking, but the officers smiled and blocked the way. Soon, a five-member SWAT team rushed onto the scene with their bulletproof shields and night sticks. They escorted me to the local police station where I was asked three questions: What is your name? Why are you here? How old are you? The police chief kindly offered me tea, and I split a package of dried Hami melon with a SWAT officer. Only after a different pair of officers escorted me to the city's central police station did anyone ask to see my photographs.

Born with an insatiable curiosity, my father, who I will identify as "Lindstrom" hereafter, first visited China in 1981. The land that invented paper and watercolor painting became a must-visit. From Guilin he rode a bicycle out into the countryside to photograph people in fields and villages, befriended locals and artists, and brought home suitcases full of Chinese rice paper to paint on. The country enchanted him. Handwriting is an art and even in the most humble homes, a painting hangs on the wall. He would later return to China to take art lessons. When I was offered a teaching position at Jilin University in Changchun, he encouraged me to go, and "experience as much as you can." I would teach English in China from 1987 to 1988, leaving a year before the dramatic democracy uprising in Tiananmen Square. I wouldn't return for more than twenty years.

Lindstrom and I shared a love of photography. He gave me my first camera, a vintage Bolsey B2 Rangefinder. I was ten, and I've owned a 35mm camera ever since. Inside the house his children grew up in, he set aside a space as a photographic darkroom. I remember the enormous enlarger, the reams of Kodak paper not to be opened in the light, fluttering negatives, trays and tongs, and the exotic smells of developer and fixer. He taped my childhood crayon "abstractions," scribbles of primary colors, just below the red safe light. The best one, he said, filled every millimeter of my paper canvas. We would spend hours in that darkroom—Lindstrom printing black and white images of Mexican streets and Utah ghost towns, using his magician-like hands to "burn" in an underexposed patch of sage or a church bell tower, and me, once I was tall enough to see over the sink, developing photos of my little brother Chris doing tricks on his bicycle or our collie dog Scotty posing nobly in front of Beutler's barn where we swung from a rope in the rafters and fell happily into the hay. Missing a wider range of color, Lindstrom would move on from black and white in the 1980s to develop color prints using the more expensive Cibachrome.

Like other proud fathers, he shot photographs of his children. Because of his training as a portrait photographer, they are generally compositional, unlike those of most other parents (figures 1, 2, 3).

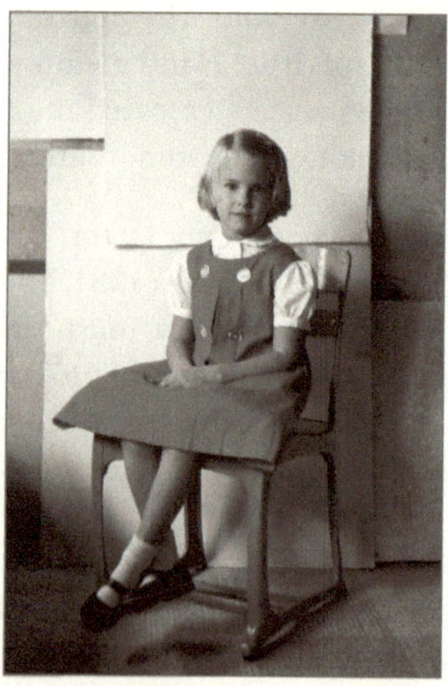

Figure 1: Lori Lindstrom, North Logan, Utah

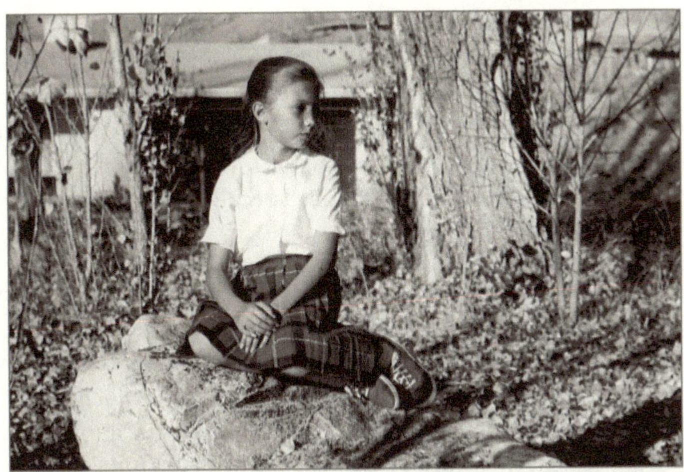

Figure 2: Leslie Lindstrom, North Logan, Utah

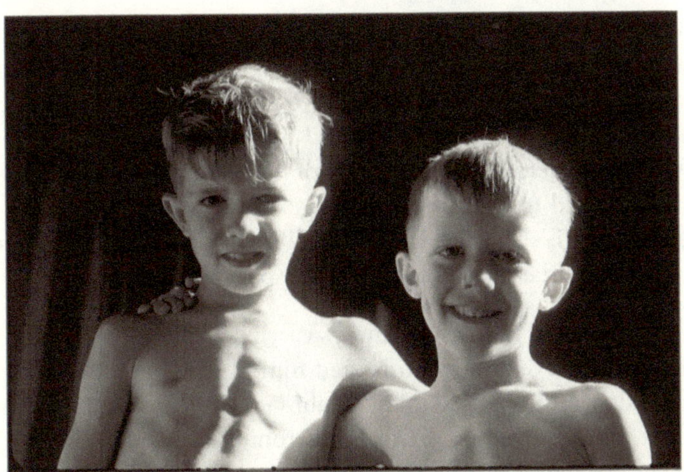

Figure 3: Braden and Chris Lindstrom, North Logan, Utah

Lindstrom especially enjoyed landscape and street photography, often in other countries. His four children waited for him to come home, his suitcases loaded with gifts. These included lederhosen, a hand-carved nutcracker sporting the head of a Brothers Grimm-like character, a Grecian coin necklace, a Mexican shawl, Icelandic boots, and Scandinavian sweaters.

He shipped his exposed Agfa film to New York for processing, putting a quarter in the bottom of the film canister, a tip for the developer. He hoped his film would jump the queue and be returned faster.

The day it came in the mail he assembled the family in the living room—off with the lights, on with the slide projector—and we were magically transported to the streets of Takayama, Oaxaca, or Rome. Lindstrom's narrative of his adventures in these strange and attractive places accompanied the beautiful images. Now the grain of his photographs have grown more pronounced with age, but I recall seeing them as a child, sharp and extraordinarily vivid.

Because of his slideshows we felt like we were growing up all over the world. Inspired, Chris and I, along with friends, would stand atop the roof of our tree house battling pirates bent on sacking Hong Kong or storm heavily-armed forts we named "Old Glory," "Tenochtitlan," and, strangely, "Alcatraz," rocky outcroppings of "Lindstrom" mountain, one of the Utah Rockies. Always victorious we would skip home through green hay fields.

Lindstrom worked professionally as a photographer for a number of years, and at one point owned a studio. Had a love for painting not called him away, this would likely have remained his career. After he closed his studio, he never seemed to work very hard on his photography, which generally was in service of his main interest, painting, but he still managed to capture images that would sell thousands of postcards through his short-lived American West postcard company and his slideshows would enthrall his children, especially me.

When traveling Lindstrom always carried a roll of dollar bills on a trip and tipped everyone who helped him in the slightest, perhaps to counterbalance the "ugly American abroad" image. We often traveled and shot photos together. With Lindstrom as a guide, I saw the Ksar of Ait Benhaddou in Morocco, a tribute to Alfred Hitchcock in Paris's Centre Pompidou (famous props from his films, including *Vertigo*'s necklace and *Rear Window*'s camera, were displayed atop purple velvet in glass cases), Walpi atop the First Hopi Mesa, Harper's Ferry, and all the national parks in Utah. We also visited Guatemala, Mexico, Sweden, and Germany. He would freely give me photography and travel advice: take two photos of an interesting subject; buy a postcard of the Colosseum as opposed to shooting precious film, unless you find a unique angle; know the rules, such as, a figure should look into the composition not out, then break them; the violation of rules can make art; spend more time in small towns because big cities are often much alike; and, skimp on hotels and entertainment, not food. "You learn how to travel," he said. The man Lindstrom always called "Grout," Harrison Groutage, his traveling-buddy and fellow watercolorist, called him "a fine traveler."[1] Part of this was his keen eye for detail. Lindstrom would draw my attention to the thickness of the dividing lines painted on the German autobahn, the door handles of a medieval church, and the black smoke of burning olive pits fueling ceramic kilns in Fez. Once, while visiting a pioneer church near the Toroweap Overlook in Arizona, he almost stepped on a rattlesnake. He recalled: "I wasn't certain it was a Diamond-back until I saw the rattles. The color was tan and black in a very beautiful pattern." The thought of being bitten and a hundred miles from a hospital was the farthest thing from his mind. Lindstrom was one of Henry James's people, someone "on whom nothing is lost," except when it came to mundane details, like finding the car. Of a second trip to fairy-tale Bamberg, Germany, he wrote: "I walked the old city and then was unable to find the car! I tried for two hours and gave up and had something to eat while the police looked for it... After an hour I was back at the station and they had found it!"

His syllabus for his art students stated: "visual training means training by which we can not only 'see' better, but to learn to also PERCEIVE. It is perception that distinguishes the extraordinary from that which is commonplace, shoddy, poorly conceived, and generally, hence, unde-sirable. A perceptive individual is one who lives better and more fully."[2] He is suggesting a recognition of beauty in all its forms. The poet Percy Shelley wrote, "it is through beauty that civilization comes." Someone who sees beauty advocates for the disadvantaged and protects the land, something Lindstrom tried to do his entire life.

If not for art he would have taught history. Ruins, including Mexico's Chichen Itza and the ancient but still occupied villages of Walpi, Arizona, held special interest because they appealed to him both artistically and historically. His personal library contained many books of history. At the end of his life he was reading Barack Obama's autobiography and the Joseph Smith papers. He delighted in telling his children about John Wesley Powell's adventures in Utah. He took me to see histor-ical movies: The beheading of Charles I in *Cromwell* was particularly traumatic. I was nine years old. Sometimes his keen interest in history took humorous turns. Thinking the film's subject was the American spy plane piloted by Gary Powers shot down over Russia, Grout and

Lindstrom bought tickets for *U2: Rattle and Hum*. They walked out just before Bono and the band performed their second number. On another occasion, while we were driving on Interstate 5 past Portland's Veterans Memorial Coliseum, Lindstrom noticed on the marquee: "CHINA SHOW." Thinking it must be a display of Chinese history or art, he took the next exit. We drove all the way back to the coliseum and walked up to an open door to see inside a large collection of china plates.

Upon returning from a solo trip abroad, I would sit with Lindstrom at the kitchen table for a critique of my photographs. He said I "had a good eye," and then suggested how the shot could be improved. "Make sure you don't cut people's feet off." I always hoped that he would create a painting from one of my photographs. And he did (figure 4). Something struck him about a group of women sitting on the steps of a church in Ouro Preto, Brazil, but I also suspect he did the painting to encourage me in my photography.

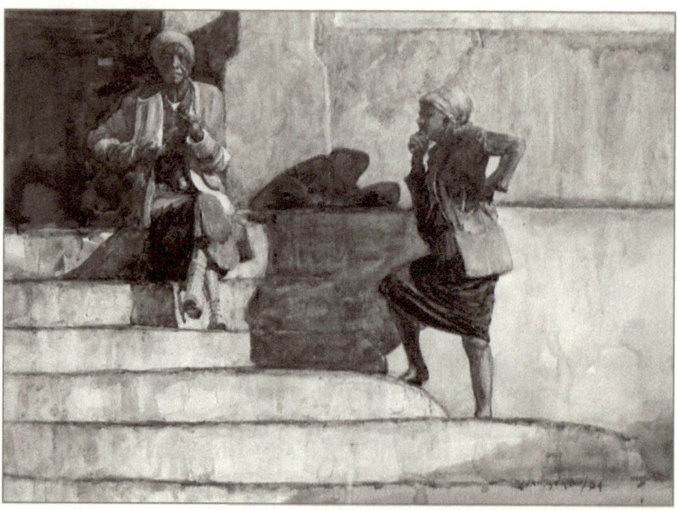

Figure 4: *Untitled*. Watercolor. 11 3/4 x 18 in. 1994

He would crop one of my prints using the white backs of other photographs to show what could be eliminated: "The first thing to do is to lose the distractions." This became a starting principle in all our discussions of art. While we were admiring a print of Gustave Caillebotte's masterpiece *Paris Street; Rainy Day* (1877), he pointed to the odd appearance of tiny legs under an umbrella in the center of the painting. I once visited the Louvre with Lindstrom (and therefore didn't need an audio guide). We miraculously found ourselves almost completely alone looking at Leonardo da Vinci's *Mona Lisa*. The conversation eventually turned to the "distractions" in the painting. Because of the similar size and color of her exposed chest, it competed for attention with her face. Also, her hands are slightly out of proportion to the rest of her body. At the time I was confused.

"This is all academic," Lindstrom whispered.

"Why is it so famous?" I said.

"The enigmatic smile, the fantastical background… it's still a great painting."

Chapter 2:

The Artist's Eye

Lindstrom thought his own work was "mostly academic," but he did experiment. He splattered canvases with rubber cement. The cement would resist the paint, creating numerous white tree branches and adding to the density of the image. He glued colored tissue paper to other canvases to give his watercolors of mining towns and urbanscapes texture and an element of abstraction. He agreed with Picasso: "Paintings are but research and experiment."

Another painter Lindstrom admired, Thomas Moran, wrote:

> *It seems to me that the bane of American art is that our artists paint for money, and repeat themselves so that in many instances you can tell the parentage of the picture that moment you look at it. It is not true that the public requires such a repetition on the part of the artist.*[3]

About his own painting philosophy, Lindstrom said: "One ought not to be too pleased with one's work, nor should one always use the same technique and materials and only change the subject. Creativity is not well served with this approach."[4] To a journalist, he said, "Instead of seeing how many different mountains you can paint the same way, see how many different ways you can paint the same mountain."[5] He painted whatever he found interesting, be it subject, color, or composition. The fact that he didn't experiment often may account for his work being little known outside of Utah. But he was a child of parents barely surviving financially, grew up in a place that had little respect for new art movements, and experienced the tutelage of a realist painter and fierce opponent of modern art. Further, through his studies he would become aware of the fact that artists who experimented were often ridiculed and starved. An 1874 exhibition of Impressionists including Auguste Renoir and Claude Monet elicited more laughter than praise.[6]

Early in their careers Monet borrowed money from Édouard Manet to pay rent[7] and buy food while Picasso couldn't afford canvas.[8] "Experiments" didn't sell, at least initially. And although Lindstrom outwardly seemed casual about selling his work, he still had a family to support.

After a year of teaching English in China, I took the Trans-Siberian Railway to Moscow, with vague plans to meet Lindstrom in Stockholm, who would fly in from the States. We had an approximate date to meet but not a specific place. Upon arriving in Sweden's capital city, I thought: Where would my father be right now? Immediately I headed for the oldest square in the city, Stortorget. Amid the men in tailored suits and Swedish models in mini-skirts pushing retro Victorian baby carriages, I noticed a man in beige trousers and an unfashionable suit coat walking away from me. I hustled up next to him and said, "Hello, Mr. Lindstrom."

The visual world could also be disappointing to Lindstrom. On this same European trip, intrigued with the history of Communism after a year in China, I was anxious to see the Berlin wall, still in use, while Lindstrom wanted to visit Brussels to see the old town. I would win out. He later wrote: "Neither the wall or checkpoint [Charlie] too impressive. Wall covered totally with graffiti & rather interesting in quantity if not quality." Back in Utah, he was especially critical of anything big and bland; this, of course, included architecture and billboards. Structures that were the largest, thus the most conspicuous, ought to be the most beautiful, he said. The remodel of Saint George's Dixie High School—its façade now a gray and dark maroon—was "a mistake." Instead, Lindstrom suggested the colors should echo the red rock of southern Utah. Further, there was little variety in many prominent buildings around the state; they were all boxes of right angles (the lighthouse in Lindstrom's 1949 painting *Eastern Point Lighthouse* tilts at such an angle that it should collapse in a heap, perhaps a visual portrayal of his crusade against right angles). Upon leaving the Louvre, Lindstrom told me it reminded him of a large warehouse. It's fair to say he thought, like Renoir:

> *We get too accustomed to these things, to such a point that we don't realize how ugly they are. And if the day ever comes when we become entirely accustomed to them, it will be the end of civilization which gave us the Parthenon and the cathedral of Rouen. Then men will all commit suicide from boredom; or else kill each*

other off, just for the pleasure of it![9]

Lindstrom was delighted to see Frank Gehry's Disney Hall in Los Angeles. He remarked, "I can't believe it," which my mother and I knew was high praise. A Utah State University (USU) colleague, who worked with him on the design of a new fine arts center on campus, called him "an artist, whose design sensibility went far beyond clay and watercolor. A man for all visual arts."[10] Even though his first job after high school, paying 50 cents an hour, was painting billboards along the highway, Lindstrom would later decry the proliferation of the monstrosities that lined Utah's scenic byways. As chairman, chief financier, and secretary of "The Committee for a More Beautiful Utah," composed mostly of immediate family members, Lindstrom wrote letters to Senator Bill Bradley, Utah's governor Norman Bangerter, and to the state's largest newspaper petitioning to have the signs removed:

> *Billboards represent greed. They represent the desire to make a buck at the expense of everything else. They represent infighting among many interests. Some say they bring more money to Utah. They do not. Every highway traveler knows there are gas stations, hotels, motels, Burger Kings... auto dealers, etc., even in small towns. Why do they have to glare at us as we try to enjoy the roads and highways we built as taxpayers?*[11]

He would agree with David Ogilvy in *Confessions of an Advertising Man*: "Man is at his vilest when he erects a billboard."[12]

Hunting was also a source of distress and a subject of another letter to the editor:

> *I understand that a bill was pushed through the Utah Legislature allowing the hunting of penned elk. Slaughter is a more accurate term. A sport is where opposing sides are somewhat equal. If there were about the same number of hunters killed as hunted killed, it might be called a "sport." But slaughtering one of God's most majestic creations is a hideous act under any circumstance.*[13]

He had this sentiment in common with Renoir, who spoke of the wealthy class: "Those imbeciles in their red hunting coats! I'd like to shoot them all! If there is a hell, they'll be hunted by deer until they drop from exhaustion!"[14]

No one I know would suggest Lindstrom was a curmudgeon, although my mother once asked if he liked anything. About a "poor" movie or restaurant, he would say: "It's not going to win a prize." He didn't care much for the film *Judgement at Nuremberg*: "I thought Spencer Tracy was very minor. He sat 90% of the time." Out of more than a thousand shots, the director of a film depicting events in early Mormon history held too long on a single shot of the moon. Lindstrom wouldn't find Hitchcock's stories ennobling, but he would admire Sir Alfred's attention to *mise en scène*. He loved Zhang Yimou's film *Not One Less*. Johannes Vermeer's painting *Girl with a Red Hat*, with its brilliant use of light, rendered Lindstrom nearly speechless: "I can't find anything wrong with it." Of course, he loved many other things: the Musée d'Orsay, Diego Velázquez's *Las Meninas*, the artist villages in the state of Oaxaca, mountains, and the sound of breaking ocean waves: "I always wanted to live by the ocean. I could sit and watch it for hours, especially in Oregon."

On a road trip to Minnesota, he drove out of his way to see Thomas Moran's painting *Shoshone Falls on the Snake River* in the Whitney Western Art Museum. "It was not a disappointment!" he exclaimed. Although everyone else in the family turned up their noses at their sight and smell, he loved the kalamata olives and goat cheese at Granatos, an Italian deli in Salt Lake City. Famously, although he didn't like any food that was "too sweet," he loved a good bakery. Every day we were in Germany, he walked to the local bakery for pastries. While visiting my sister Leslie in Pennsylvania, they drove to an Amish bakery. He was set on buying a loaf of apple bread. Leslie recalls: "When I told him that maybe he would like something else considering how expensive the loaf was, he employed his characteristic long pause, then replied, 'That may be, but I only plan on buying one loaf in my life.'" In Honolulu, while traveling with my student friends from BYU-Hawai'i and myself, he sat at a table inside the beautiful, open-air atrium of a 5-star hotel, where he planned to treat us to fruit juice. "Dad," I whispered, "you can buy drinks cheap at the ABC store around the corner." He said, "Braden, it's not about the drinks."

For Christmas one year, Lindstrom gave me the book *Vincent van Gogh: Letters from Provence*, writing inside the front cover: "Here's a different kind of literature, unique and great!" Lindstrom greatly admired the Dutch painter. They were alike in several ways: health struggles, an acute sense of sight, a passion for the natural world, and an innate modesty. From Arles, van Gogh wrote to his brother Theo, "Oh, how I wish you could see all that I am seeing these days. I can only let myself go with so many lovely things in front of me, especially as I think that the work is getting somewhat better..."[15]

It was no coincidence, then, that one afternoon Lindstrom and I stood looking at a van Gogh painting in the Los Angeles County Museum of Art. He asked me where my eye went first. I said, to the small figure of a man in the painting. Why? Because I can relate to a person in a painting. Lindstrom replied, the human figure becomes the most dominant because you expect action, movement. "Man is the measure of all things," he said, quoting Protagoras. Many of Lindstrom's works depict moving or stationary people, although he always felt uncomfortable portraying the human face. In his paintings of people on the streets in Mexico selling their wares or produce to eke out a living, there are echoes of Jean-Francois Millet's farmworkers, of which, Renoir said: "His sentimental peasants made me think of actors dressed up to look like peasants."[16] Even Lindstrom, who enjoyed Millet's work, told me that the Frenchman's paintings were a "little sweet."

Many of the human subjects in Lindstrom's paintings are also the working poor, while the colors are often bright and beautiful, for example, the K'iche' Maya women on the steps of the church of Santo Tomás in Guatemala, and a man carrying a pot on his head to a Mexican market. In most of his paintings the streets are swept free of dirt and garbage. At first glance, casual viewers might see Lindstrom's work as more closely resembling Millet's *The Gleaners* than van Gogh's *The Potato Eaters*. On closer inspection, they will note the shadows, dark and distorted backgrounds, and burdened faces. Perhaps Millet and Lindstrom are saying to the world, using its own standards, that the people in the paintings are beautiful. There is beauty in the fields and streets. One has to be curious enough to look, and trained to see. "I will confess," Lindstrom wrote, "that sometimes I wish I could project myself into other people's lives so that I may feel more than simply the outward dressings." But I believe he had, as William Wordsworth wrote about poets, "a greater power to think and feel." His Chinese art professor friend in Hangzhou, Fan Xiaoming, wrote of his paintings, "I don't see many artworks nowadays which express such a deep sympathy and tender feeling of ordinary people and nature in the artist's whole life."[17]

The values in Lindstrom's oeuvre are often dark, but are usually contrasted with light. Dr. Vern Swanson, the former curator of the Springville Art Museum (Utah), wrote:

> *Dissatisfied with the "don't do" restrictions and the pretty delicacy of most of the J.A.F. Everett school, [Lindstrom] began experimenting with paint—how dark his pigments could go, how many layers could be laid down, and how off-color his hues could be and still comprise a workable watercolor. "I wanted," he explained, "to get the guts back into Utah watercolor painting again!"[18]*

Above the men in Lindstrom's *Wall Street Journal* is an enormous weeping wall, speckled with red. Swaths of paint, like the aftermath of a rain storm, fall in no discernable pattern, staining the wall, leaving behind jagged streaks of grey, pale blue, and black. But puncturing the stains are tiny strips of white lace swirl above the fedora of one man sitting on the maroon bench. His high-collared laborer's shirt catches ribbons of sunlight, created by leaving slices of the canvas unpainted. At his knees, he rests a newspaper, the columns of print and photos a washout. The newspaper, as if it hides a source of light, is translucent and bright, a startling contrast to the dark values of the rest of the painting.

As he aged, Lindstrom's curiosity grew; even in retirement, he was never bored. Film critic Roger Ebert wrote: "A civilized man is a person whose curiosity [about other people] outweighs his prejudices..."[19] With his affable manner and curiosity about everything and everyone, Lindstrom easily made friends all over the world. I was often the beneficiary: an art professor in Hong Kong treated me to a lavish, five-course meal; a couple in Greenwich Village invited me in for tea and conversation, mainly about the artist; in the dead of winter, a waitress he befriended in Guilin, China convinced her boyfriend to let me stay for free in his apartment, which boasted a small space heater running on hijacked electricity; and a Salt Lake City auto mechanic, whom Lindstrom employed to fix my car's smashed rear end (courtesy of a drunk driver), said, "I deal with a lot of people in this business. I've never met anyone more honest than your father." When I picked up the used car it looked brand new.

His curiosity was not always reciprocated. Fascinated by the enormous panoramic photographs of a Hanapepe, Kauai photographer, Lindstrom visited his shop multiple times in a 24-hour period to talk with him about cameras, film, panoramic prints, etc. Recognizing a curious non-buyer, the photographer rolled his eyes. After the first visit to the shop, my mother and I pretended to be busy with a map, watching from the car as Lindstrom walked back inside. Once, when waiting at the airport for our flight from Guatemala City to the United States, a woman sat next to Lindstrom and struck up a conversation. Always eager to make a new friend, he happily talked with her while, unbeknownst to him, her accomplice stole his carry-on bag containing his cameras and all the video footage he had shot of perfect conical volcanoes, pristine lakes, and the colorful market of Chichicastenango. He sighed and wondered if his insurance would replace the camera.

Lindstrom's life was sometimes a paradox . At the kitchen table he would expound at length on Utah history and then claim to know very little. His southern Utah landscapes are representational while mysterious vapors swirl around his imagined, Chinese-inspired mountains. Lindstrom wasn't happy, and was even discouraging, when I postponed my dissertation work at the University of Hawai'i to focus on writing and directing a short narrative film based on a local folktale. This caught me by surprise—I was trying to make a piece of art myself. "You need to finish your degree to secure a position," he said.

He worried about money, but never balanced a checkbook and camped overnight at a hotel despite invitations to stay with family and friends. If staying with the latter was one's only option, "always under-stay your welcome," he told me.

He was a child of the Great Depression and had a highly practical mother, his most important tutor, yet he was an artist with ambition in a crowded field. This binary must have been a source of tension throughout his life.

Chapter 3:

Life with Dad

At home, Lindstrom often seemed to be "missing." He would sequester himself in front of an easel in the basement, later in his studio, a space separate from the rest of the house. His daughter Leslie remembers trips as a young child to the basement to visit him. He would be drawing a figure, sometimes a nude, based on a projected photographic slide. At the sound of her footfalls, he turned off the projector, said hello, and then patiently listened to the joys and travails of a little girl growing up in rural Utah.

Although he generally liked sports, he never watched one of my brother's little league football games or any of my high school tennis matches. Generally, this didn't bother us. We always assumed he was busy. On one occasion when he did come to the gym to watch me coach a high school basketball game, he left at half-time because he thought the game was over.

Our family was in many ways typical of others in the neighborhood: white, middle-class, Latter-Day Saints, with more kids than the U.S. average. Like everyone else on our block, my siblings and I attended public schools, struggled to sit still in church, dined on bologna and Miracle Whip sandwiches, and threw snowballs at cars. But unlike everyone else, we regularly visited every art museum along the Wasatch Front, climbed cathedral-high pink sand dunes in southern Utah, and sucked on horehound candy during intermission at the Utah Shakespeare Festival.

Despite his children's follies, Lindstrom was always congenial. When my sister Lori was a teenager and broke curfew one evening, returning home well after midnight, she found Lindstrom waiting for her. There was no reprimand, just concern that she was alright amid worries about the dangers that lurk in the dark for teenagers. When bored, Chris and

I liked to play with matches and one afternoon accidentally set fire to a field. He taught us about consequences. He once took us to a hospital in Long Beach, California. On the way we complained about missing time at Disneyland, but Lindstrom insisted. We visited his childhood friend Alonzo, who contracted polio after World War II and had been hospitalized ever since, breathing with the assistance of an iron lung. Taped on Alonzo's nightstand was this thought: "We were put on earth not to see through people, but to see people through."

Lindstrom often talked of John Wesley Powell. I think he envied Powell and his adventures. Although the world had been mapped, there was much of it Lindstrom had never seen, and so he was never at a loss in finding other roads to travel. As Matthew Bevis wrote about the poet John Ashbery, Lindstrom was "rooted and en route,"[20] loaded with cameras (my mother would say, "his camera was attached to his hip!"), several lenses, and large format, 4 x 5 inch film or multiple rolls of 35mm. On sabbatical in Greece, he brought equipment with him so he could immediately develop photos "to see what he was getting." The *Salt Lake Tribune* wrote that he had "visited practically every pioneer settlement and ghost town in southern Utah and Nevada."[21] He was the American photographer navigating Suzhou's canals or the explorer wandering Baja fishing villages with Grout. On that trip Grout returned alone to Utah while Lindstrom lingered, finding his own way back across the border. He wrote his daughter Leslie in March, 1975: "Sometimes I just like to go alone and take a few pictures or draw a little bit."

While Lindstrom was away my mother stayed home to watch the kids. One year she decided it was her turn to go to Europe and paid for a seat on a group tour. Lindstrom told her he had to teach USU extension courses in Moab and Vernal, Utah the same week she would be gone. Upset, she was about to cancel, but he insisted she go. When he was a teenager, on at least one occasion, both of his parents would leave him home alone for weeks. In 1938 his father wrote, "My Dear Gale—How are you getting along as a bachelor! Are you able to boil water without [scorching] it?... I am sending you five dollars to live on for another week." My mother almost backed out of her first European trip, but at the last minute decided to go, putting Leslie in charge. She was 16 and had a driver's license. While the parents were away, the kids, of course, decided to go to the movies. Lindstrom grew up watching movies and the medium appealed to his interests in sound and image. My mother always remembered seeing *The Wizard of Oz* at the age of ten in a small Pioche, Nevada theater. After her father passed away, she often accompanied her mother on trips to the movie theater at the MGM hotel in Las Vegas where she fell in love with musicals, especially those starring Esther Williams. After my siblings and I pooled our money, we came up just short for the four of us to go to a drive-in theater. The logical thing to do was to hide someone on the back seat, but the only one brave enough was Lori, the tallest of the siblings. So we buried her with blankets and the ticket seller waved us in.

My mother deserves enormous credit for taking care of affairs at home, allowing Lindstrom to travel and practice his art; as the reader will see, the one facilitated the other. He would drive or fly to some distant place, take pictures, return, teach school all day, and come home to paint for two to three hours at night. Art, according to my mother, was "as important to him as air to breathe. It has to be," she continued, "if you want to be any good at it." Lindstrom's mentor and friend, Chen Chi, wrote about the development of a landscape painter:

> *In addition to the technical development, there must be knowledge for the understanding of nature. You must read 10,000 volumes of the classics and travel 10,000 miles to absorb the spirit of the great mountains and rivers. Then you paint of your knowledge and experience. The eye, the mind, and the material must become one in painting.*[22]

It's clear Lindstrom struggled to balance a quest for beauty and commitment to his art with a devotion to family. Van Gogh would write to his mother: "If one has taken all the pains to master the brush, *one cannot leave painting alone.*"[23]

We ask painters, why do you paint? "Sometimes I wonder," questioned Graham Greene, "how all those who do not write, compose or paint can manage to escape the madness, the melancholia, the panic fear which is inherent to the human condition." Painting was an escape for Lindstrom, but it was also something else. He saw beauty in all its forms as a counterweight and painted to contribute his part. As Toni Morrison wrote, "Beauty was not simply something to behold; it was something one could do."

When I would accompany him on a road trip, before leaving town, the first stop was always at a gas station to clean the windshield. The better to see. On the road, when we got near a semi-truck, because it blocked the view, he'd power by. He never liked to drive at night. Sometimes when driving together we had no particular destination in mind; Lindstrom would say, "Let's go there and see what we can see." Most often the pursuit was benign, but sometimes it was dangerous. Once, while admiring the view as he drove us in a station wagon along a reservoir in northern Utah, mountains on one side, water on the other, he wandered into the opposite lane, recovering just in time to miss an oncoming car. I envisioned the newspaper headline: "Utah Artist Spots Doe and Dies."

When Leslie was two years old she sat on Mom's lap in a Plymouth convertible for a slow drive up Cedar Mountain in southern Utah. It was a gorgeous day, the sun lighting up the red and yellow leaves of autumn trees. Lindstrom pointed out the colors to Leslie and Mom gently protested, "She's too young to understand." He replied, "She's not too young to appreciate beauty." On another road trip, this one through his favorite part of California, he wrote: "Wheat was ripe and ready to cut in the Sacramento Valley. Here in the city it is warm and some fog is coming through the Golden Gate. I have been here dozens of times but it is as though each were the first." I recall his visit to the National Museum of the American Indian in Washington, D.C. Lindstrom was one of its first eager patrons when it opened in 2004. Stunned by the faces of Allan Houser's sculptures, Lindstrom remarked, the works were "so beautiful they make you weep." I had never seen Lindstrom cry other than when he annually played "The Twelve Days of Christmas" on the piano and we would all sing along, our voices joyously yawping every time we hit the fifth day. Lindstrom always laughed so hard he cried but somehow managed to keep his fingers playing.

To his family Lindstrom was never too high or too low. When someone was having a meltdown, he said, "Don't get all bent out of shape." Usually people paused to figure out what this meant, which gave them a moment to calm down. The literary character that comes the closest to Lindstrom is Atticus Finch. Like the Alabama lawyer, there was always a quiet dignity about him as he explored the world.

As a child I never thought it unusual that Lindstrom was away and I didn't know when he would be home. My friends' fathers never seemed to go anywhere. Similar to the protagonist in Graham Greene's short story, "A Shocking Accident," who "recreated his father—from a restless widowed author into a mysterious adventurer who travelled in far places" and believed "his father either 'ran guns' or was a member of the British Secret Service," I envisioned my father as a world-renowned explorer.

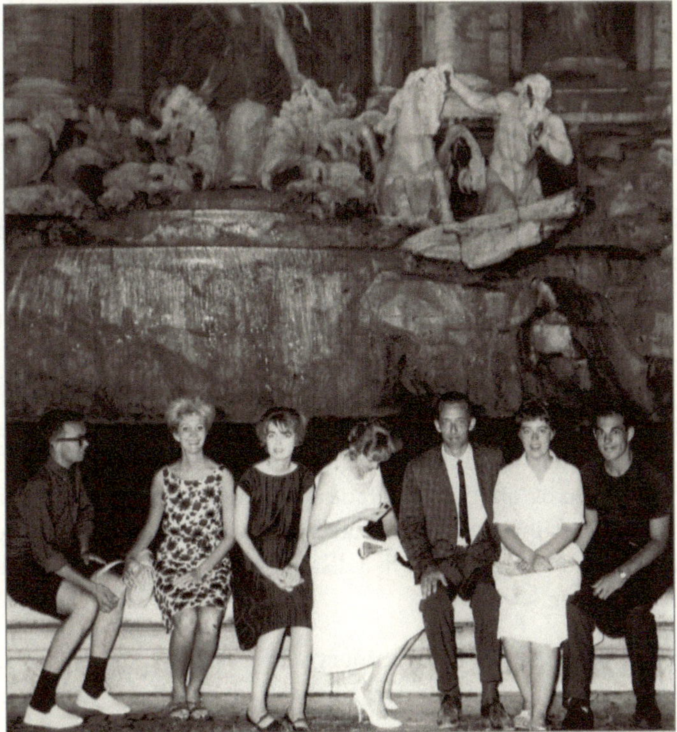

Figure 5: Lindstrom (3rd from right), 1969 World Academy Tour, Rome

When I knew he was abroad, using a stolen key, I would sneak into his studio, which replaced the basement as a workshop. Looking back on those years, I suppose he knew of these covert visits and didn't mind, in fact, encouraged them by often leaving the door unlocked. As the resident magician and interested in all things magic, Lindstrom filled his studio with objects of interest, especially to a young boy. I suspect he grew weary of surrounding himself with flat, two-dimensional drawings and paintings, so many of the discoveries in the studio were three-dimensional: African masks, Hopi baskets, bamboo paint brushes, a Spanish ceramic bull, and Japanese fish kites. At first, I looked for the Civil War swords, most often stashed in a closet high above my head.

As I grew older and my furtive visits continued, I began to seek out the latest painting on his easel. One day a canvas might boast the image of a face, the next day a shoulder and torso, then hands would appear. It was like watching a black and white photograph develop, only slower. I rarely saw Lindstrom actually paint. Yet the full image of a person would finally appear, as if conjured from the air. He once explained his technique to a magazine reporter:

> *Lindstrom says he is different in that he paints his pictures in parts or pieces. He finishes a part of the picture before he goes on to the next part. You may have to make some adjustments at the end, but he pretty much does this in his work as he goes along. He admits that it is difficult with this method to get the painting to hang together and not look like a patchwork quilt.*[24]

Lindstrom was an exacting painter, and never a prolific one, producing perhaps ten watercolors a year, according to his friend Vern Swanson.[25] Upon finishing a painting, if something didn't work, he either wouldn't sign his name to it or he would throw it away. He was always his most demanding critic. To a gallery owner, he wrote in 2001: "Today I worked on another watercolor (Chinese subject), likely another rather average painting unless it starts looking better very soon. About the only thing one can salvage in a disappointing watercolor is the other side of the paper."

Lindstrom rarely did a preliminary study. "I would rather just do the painting." It was certainly faster. I believe he enjoyed finishing, more than starting a piece. This may explain why he never did an extraordinarily large canvas with the exception of the enormous murals in several buildings on the USU campus. But those were collaborative efforts with his colleagues, Ev Thorpe and Grout, assisted by art students. Lindstrom was also a modest man, and the "small" size of his paintings reflect this. Note the modifiers in his explanation of why he focused on watercolors:

> *I tried a number of other media and somewhat settled on watercolor as being a little more interesting for me than perhaps oil painting. I had sort of a difficult time with oil paints at first and probably still do, however. I wasn't sure quite how to go about it. I didn't know whether you put the paint on thick or thin or quite what to paint on….*

Watercolor painting is quite exciting. And one, so to speak, must move along, corrections or major changes are not possible, so it was more of a challenge, I suppose, than oil painting—you could paint forever on the same painting in oils and perhaps end up with something reasonable or maybe not. But with watercolor you sort of had to come up with something within a reasonable amount of time. That and the fact that watercolor paint... has a luminosity because one could look through the paint and onto the white paper and get an entirely different result than with oil paint that usually was opaque or... could be painted thinly, I suppose.[26]

One evening we watched a documentary film about Leonardo da Vinci. In a memorable scene, the actor playing da Vinci strolls into his studio, thoughtfully peers at a canvas, makes a single brush stroke, and then leaves, in effect calling it a day. At the time I thought: That's just like our resident artist! My young mind wondered if Lindstrom's way of working was an homage to the great Italian artist. It's clear that the demands of teaching, traveling, family, and friends interrupted his art. But I suspected there were additional factors at play—the difficulty of painting with watercolors, the constant search to express something in a new way, and an incessant feeling, especially in his later years, that "I am not getting any better—likely the opposite," as he wrote to an artist friend in 2005, at age 85.

Chapter 4:

A Sense of Wonder

Although on some occasions my siblings and I felt we were in class listening to a college lecture, Lindstrom measured his words even when trying to be funny. Generally, if it could be said in five words instead of six, he would say it in four. Rarely flippant and almost always to the point when he spoke, his words were carefully hewn. What the film-maker Jean Renoir wrote about his father, Auguste, is true of mine: He "would have given his life for his children without hesitation. But he was extremely reticent about revealing his private feelings to anyone—even to himself, perhaps."[27] As a child, Leslie once asked our mother, "Why doesn't Dad ever tell me he loves me?" Mom replied, "He may not be able to say it in words, but look at the other ways he expresses his love for you." Leslie looked and the question never bothered her again.

In one of his artist's statements, he noted, "I find it difficult to talk about my paintings. I hope not to produce paintings that require words," and "I believe aesthetic experiences are often enhanced by sharing. Sharing not with words necessarily, but simply by being in the presence of someone seemingly having the same experience."[28] In this he was like Edward Hopper, who wrote: "If I could say it in words there would be no reason to paint." Perhaps with a wife, four chatty children, a constantly running television, and lively collie dogs at home, Lindstrom didn't have many opportunities to talk. But of course, it's more complicated. Of the many hours he spent alone painting, he sometimes lamented that the work didn't "involve other people." However, he would probably agree with da Vinci, who argued that "the painter must be solitary especially when he is intent on those speculations and considerations, which if they are kept continually before the eyes give the memory the opportunity of mastering them. For if you are alone you are completely yourself but if you are accompanied by a single companion you are only half yourself."[29] The painter Jamie Wyeth stated: "Unlike any other [art] discipline, painting is the most individual. It's a stick with some hair on its end, and some sticky stuff you apply to a piece of cloth. With music you need an orchestra. But painting is very simple and very individual."[30] Lindstrom silently studied the details of an image, usually one of his photographs, then attempted to render them in an artful way on canvas. His professional life seeped into his personal one.

Among Lindstrom's papers, I found an article he had saved for over fifty years. Published in *Reader's Digest*, titled "Hold Fast to Wonder!", it contained this story:

> *In Japan, guests are invited to celebrate the birth of roses in a garden. An American friend of mine once went to the office of a Kyoto businessman and was kept waiting five minutes. A secretary apologized for her boss. "Please understand, a blossom on his desk has just opened, and he must contemplate it."*[31]

Lindstrom approached the natural world in the same way, and at times his enthusiasm spilled out. He drove us to national parks and monuments that he called "super spectacular!" (Of course, this was not an exaggeration. In fact, I never heard Lindstrom exaggerate.) If we were reading a book or otherwise not paying attention, he would say: "Look out the window." I always thought being asked to close a book was odd, since he was a well-read academic (his artistic philosophy and art were certainly influenced by his voracious reading and study), but in hindsight it makes perfect sense. The real world trumped all. At times when we drove past an interesting natural formation, he would slide into a lesson: "That's what we call an 'escarpment.' Rain erodes the rock, sharpening the slope."

A 1960 issue of the *Ford Times*, the motor company's monthly magazine, published a painting, photographs, and an article[32] by Lindstrom about Zion National Park. Of great interest to Lindstrom was the story of the Flanagan brothers, Dave and Will, who "built an ingenious device of telegraph wires and pulleys" to transport timber from atop Cable Mountain (the neighbor of the famed Great White Throne in Zion) to the canyon floor, some 2700 feet. "On one trip up the mountainside... Will Flanagan carried a hundred pounds of wire on his back— plus the usual thirty-five-pound pack of food. Are there many men like that around today?" I remember hearing many times the story of these men who, for fun, slid down the cable. As a child I would look up at Cable Mountain in terror.

Our family trips also included "spontaneous" detours to a gallery or museum. He would tell us: "It's not that people don't appreciate art. It's that people don't know how to see. When you learn to look at the world, then you see the beauty in the world." One way to see something, Lindstrom believed, is to draw it. Monet credits his mentor Johan Barthold Jongkind for "the final education of my eye."[33] Holding a pomegranate, Lindstrom encouraged Leslie to look at how beautiful the red is on the outside. Most people simply cut open the fruit without appreciating its color or shape.

Lindstrom was modest to a fault. He offered to help me with my dissertation, so I sent him Louise Rosenblatt's book on transactional analysis. After a few weeks, he wrote back: "I have returned your book... I am so sorry I did you no good. All I can say is that some people are SO educated they have lost their ability to communicate with ignornt [sic] people like me." I once gave him a book on the great buildings of the world. "Thank you for the excellent book," he wrote. "I have read quite a few descriptions and, of course, hope that I can remember enough to help me appear better than the dummy I really am. Much to learn..." I recognize him in the saying of the Chinese philosopher, Lao Tzu: "The wise man is one who knows what he does not know."

Chapter 5:

Our North Logan Home

Along with my mother, Lindstrom always situated the family in beautiful places and filled our homes with art. They would raise their children in North Logan, Utah. For the duration of our childhood, the town remained predominantly white, middle-class, conservative, and bucolic. Our neighbors were technology and agricultural professors, bookstore managers, bankers, mink farmers, and cattle breeders. My siblings and I decorated our trikes and bicycles with paper streamers and rode them in the July 24th Pioneer Day parade, the biggest event of the month celebrating, what I thought in my young mind, was the day Mormon pioneers won our independence from England. There were five seasons—counting winter twice. Although North Logan, originally named "Greenville" because of its many trees planted along the roads, was first settled in 1890, less than 800 people were living there in 1960 when our family moved from a duplex rental in Logan to a house modeled on one in Seattle, as first seen in an issue of *Good Housekeeping*. Before building, my parents drove to Washington state to see the house in 3D. In evoking his version of a family home, Lindstrom acted as primary contractor. Pressed for

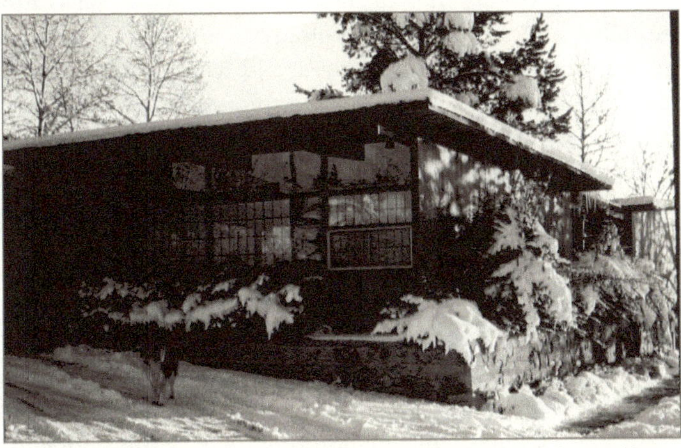

Figure 6: Lindstrom's North Logan Home

funds, he took countless trips to Anderson Lumber in Logan to ask questions so he could do much of the work himself, although he did employ Utah State University electricians and plumbers. Unlike almost every house in the neighborhood, ours sat squarely in a north-south direction, letting sunlight strike and warm the bulk of it throughout the day. The north roof flared slightly upward, opening up the house's front face, allowing Lindstrom to install large studio windows, which faced the driveway. Atop the studio he put in two skylights to extend the hours he could work, especially on overcast and winter days. He preferred to paint in natural light.

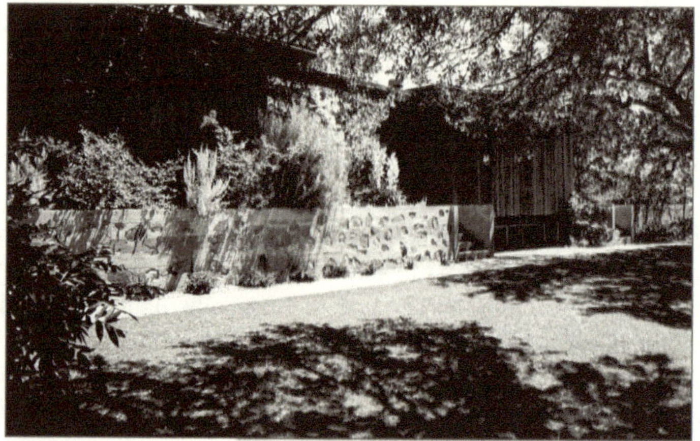

Figure 7: Lindstrom Home, West Side

An arbor of maple trees framed our gravel driveway. Scotty, then Dusty, another collie, chased their brownish-black tails around a Russian olive, and red delicious apple trees. The branch of an ancient Poplar snapped away in my eight-year-old hand, leading to a broken arm and popularity at school. Aspens, mountain ash, and yew trees. Sumac, yucca, pyracantha, sand cherry, and sage rose untamed. Ivy crept down a mound towards a patch of bluegrass. Wild asparagus sprouted in the front yard. In autumn, white and pink blossoms of pear, apple, and flowering plum trees dotted the view. Lindstrom planted a romantic garden and it grew into an impressionist landscape.

Visitors to the house would see the studio first before traveling down a long, redwood-sided breezeway towards the front door, past a Japanese garden on the right with a pedestal lantern, and flora that turned bright red and orange in autumn. The way was dark enough to attract bats, who camped for up to a fortnight before being chased away by my broom-wielding mother, to the delighted squeals of her children and their friends hiding behind a screen door. On the north and west sides of the house, a concrete foundation wall was inlaid with generous amounts of reddish sandstone, adding color and texture to what otherwise would be a smooth slab of gray (figure 7). In laying the stone, dust burned Lindstrom's eyes, causing the first of several vision scares. On the south or back side of the house, more large windows faced Logan and the Wellsville Mountains to the southwest, often topped with snow as late as June. The winter temperatures drove feral cats to crawl up onto a warm car engine block, their screeches shocking an unsuspecting Lindstrom when he tried to start the car in the morning. Herds of deer would wander down from the east mountains to snack on a golf-green-sized backyard. Lindstrom wrote in his journal in February, 1989: "One day last week there were 13 deer just outside the door. Often they come right to the windows and look into the house." For Lindstrom they were a source of great delight. The food he gave them encouraged more visits. We raised deer, not grass.

Below the south windows were square panels, white and red, bordered by dark-stained wood like a Piet Mondrian abstract, running in a row east to west. Similar panels appeared on the front of the house, creating a kind of visual symmetry (figure 8) and raising the eyebrows of curious tax assessors and meter readers. The reflections of mountains and trees in the south windows would fool birds into believing an unobstructed jet stream continued through the living room. Many times the family jumped at the sudden "BANG" of a robin that struck a window at 30 MPH. The glass survived, but the birds wouldn't.

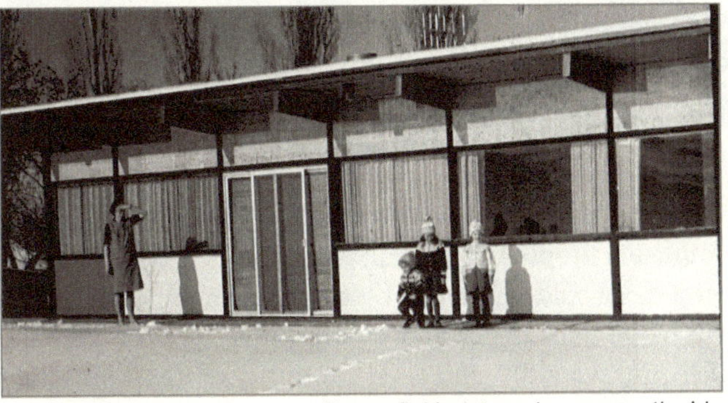

Figure 8: Lindstrom house, south side

Stepping through the front door, visitors met a gypsum rock wall, nudging them to go right into the living room or left into the dining room, the two separated by an L-shaped wall. Lindstrom designed the house so one wouldn't immediately step into the living room. Further, this room was not an extension of the dining room. There was a space for talking and another for eating. The upstairs also sported a large Japanese lantern that illuminated the stairs to the basement, and shoji doors that slid open to reveal a bedroom or office.

Artwork filled the house: Navajo rugs; Mexican black pottery; Huichol yarn paintings; an Ev Thorpe abstract oil that, as a child, I imagined was a man with a bulbous chest wearing a suit and top hat astride a horse; Lindstrom's watercolors of junks in Aberdeen Harbor, Hong Kong; an Alvin Gittins portrait of Lindstrom as a young man, holding a block flute; and an elegant baby grand piano. Lindstrom's tastes in home decoration were narrow: they ran from something beautiful to something beautiful. If he saw a piece and knew it would look good in the house and might help the artist who created it, he bought it. If questioned about affordability, he'd reply: "I'll sell a painting… or two."

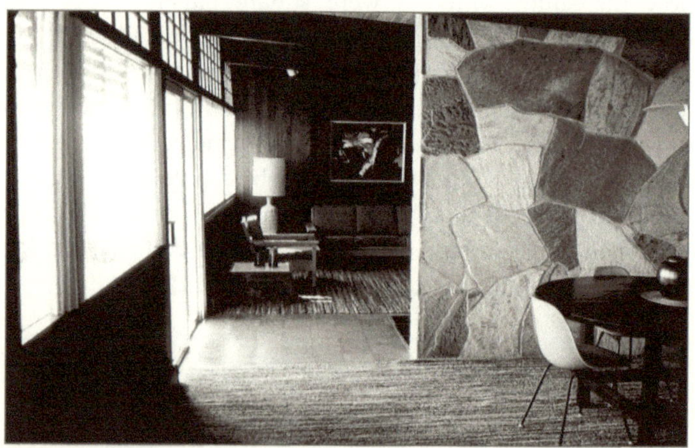
Figure 9: Lindstrom dining and living room

The house was a place of warmth and peace. Warmth also emanated from an unusual fireplace, free-standing, rounded, with no right angles. In the winter we folded purple, blue, violet, orange, and white tissue paper, cut out tiny triangles and squares, unfolded the paper to reveal snowflakes, no two alike, and then gently taped them onto the chilled, south-facing windows (figure 10).

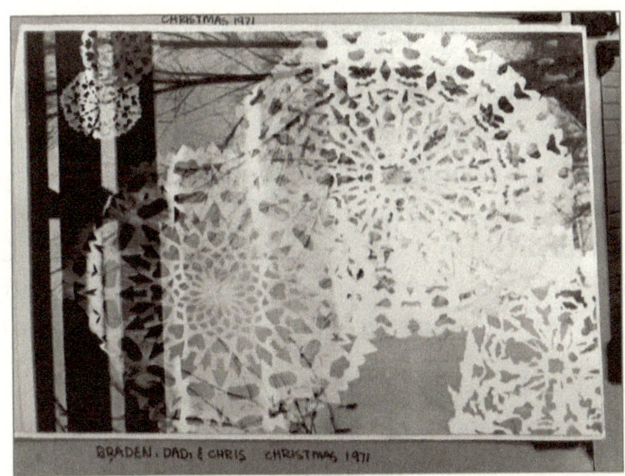

Figure 10: Snowflakes

The basement, the space where the kids played tag and wiffle ball, once hosted a Lindstrom show. "People and Places" became the title of his one-man photography exhibit of China, complete with museum-quality lighting installed just before the show opened. The photos, mounted below center on long, narrow mat board, looked like Chinese scrolls. In this underground hallway, holding cups of fruit punch and Scottish shortbread, professors and community art aficionados, along with well-dressed neighbors, gazed at the photographs and chatted Lindstrom up. The unassuming artist, dressed in corduroy, beige and brown, and slightly frayed, might have been mistaken for a small-town librarian. Through the years the family would tease him for his dated and merely functional fashions; odd, considering the beauty of his home and work. Like Renoir, he would wear the same clothes for a decade or longer.[34]

He wrote of his experience being back in Guilin, China three years after his first visit and being recognized by the waitress at the Osman-thus Hotel. "Even the clerk at the desk recognized me and spoke to me and even remembered which room I stayed in in May 1981! There must be something about me—perhaps my bad general looks makes one remember."

But he was handsome, as the two photographs here illustrate. One is a black and white, chiaroscuro portrait. Lindstrom is 19 years old (figure 11). A key-light illuminates the side of a piano, Lindstrom's right hand is lightly placed on the keys. His sensitive, young face looks down.

A single fill light falls on the bust of a composer, probably Beethoven (an idol), and a resting left hand, reflected in the shine of the piano case. His mother always thought he might become a concert pianist. He loved the "Three Bs": Bach, Beethoven, and Brahms. Classical music, in Lindstrom's opinion, was "edifying, uplifting, ennobling, like great paintings." Lindstrom was fond of quoting a verse from Mormon scripture: "seek ye out of the best books words of wisdom" (*Doctrine and Covenants* 88:118). For him, "best books," meant the best of everything in life, including the arts. "You don't have time for anything else," he told me.

"He looks like Errol Flynn!" people have remarked about a photograph of Lindstrom painting (see figure 12), his shadow looming larger than his six-foot frame. He stands in front of an unseen easel, hair slicked back (in my recollection, he always wore his hair like this), the whisper of a mustache, dapper in pleated pants, suspenders, an open-collared white shirt, sleeves rolled up, ready to drop the brush and duel saboteurs. He could be mistaken for a young Flynn. Lindstrom said of himself that he had a "swarthy appearance."

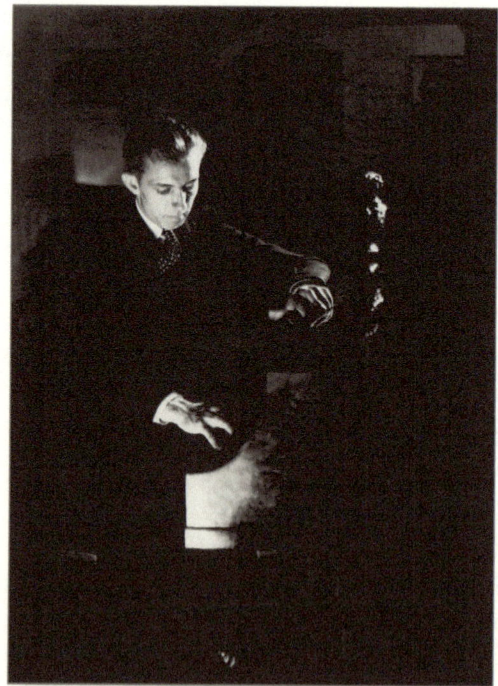

Figure 11: Salt Lake City, 1938

44

Chapter 6:

LINDSTROM & OTHER ARTISTS

Lindstrom championed fellow artists. In 1958 he promoted the National Invitational Art Exhibition at USU and headed the National Ceramic Exhibition in Logan a year later. In his travels he befriended many artists including Angelo Garzio, Fannie Nampeyo, Doña Rosa, Harry Leith-Ross, Edith Hamlin, Koo Mei, Nan McKinnel, Chen Chi, Cheng-Khee Chee, and Joseph Mugnaini (who illustrated many of Ray Bradbury's books), and invited several to present workshops at the university. When I traveled, Lindstrom encouraged me to buy something from the local artists, even some small craft children might make. "Help the kids with a purchase or two," he wrote to me. "You can always give them to the next batch of kids thereby making two groups happy."

About selling his own work, he rarely displayed it in a gallery, believing the commissions were too high. He more often showed his work in public exhibitions. He was never a self-promoter; buyers would see a piece in a show or learn of his work through others and then contact him directly. He said, "I do it [paint] because I enjoy it. I think doing it for a living would have taken the pleasure out of it."[35] Still, there were a few laments about not selling more work. One of his doctors mentioned he only bought the paintings of dead artists. With exasperation, Lindstrom told me that this didn't help anyone, the dead or the living. In a prophetic letter, van Gogh wrote to Theo, "I cannot help it that my pictures do not sell. Nevertheless the time will come when people will see that they are worth more than the price of paint."[36] I asked Lindstrom, towards the end of his life, about regrets and he said he wished he had made a little more money, then, with his characteristic shrug, said, "so it goes."

In 1983, near the end of his career, he gave the 68th Faculty Honor Lecture at USU. His title: "Thomas Moran in Utah."[37] I remember the audible gasps from the audience when Lindstrom

45

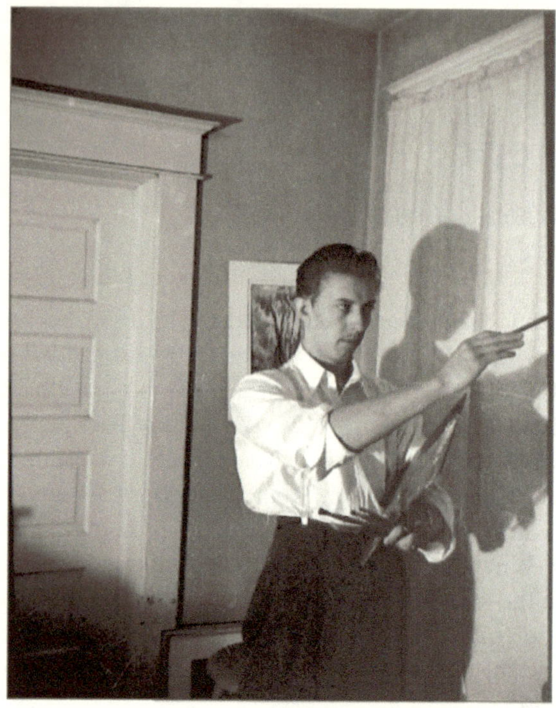

Figure 12: Salt Lake City, 1940s

projected slides of Moran landscapes, "epic in size and concept," the paintings faithful to their subjects but also grander and impressionistic. In 1872, the *Atlantic Monthly* noted: "We believe we are right in saying that this picture [*Grand Canyon of the Yellowstone*] introduces Mr. Thomas Moran to the public: it is his first important work... He must be compared with men more known, —with Church and Bierstadt; there are no others with whom it would be worthwhile to compare him." Interestingly, in his published lecture, Lindstrom quotes Moran's daughter Ruth, who says about her father, "he was never at any time interested in making any money, and always was the worst possible salesman for his pictures; almost anyone could get a picture cheapened in price, if he would only stay long enough in his studio, for my father was always aching to get back to work..." Then Lindstrom concluded the lecture pointing out that there are few Moran pieces in Utah. As reasons he suggested that Moran came to draw, not to sell his work, that "American tastes were generally turning toward European art," and that at the turn of the century, Utah's economy didn't enable the accumulation of wealth.

Late in the nineteenth century, the *Salt Lake Herald* took Utahns to task:

> *Over a hundred good pictures have been on exhibition in this city during the past week... Only two in a thousand of our population have entered the doors since they were thrown open to the public. Some veritable gems of landscape painting... are being offered at $6 a piece—original studies, carefully painted, of scenes in the neighborhood of this city. Up to this writing only two small pictures have been sold...*
>
> *Why, more people spent 25 cents to see a rocky minstrel show at a second-class theatre last week than have paid to see a collection of one hundred and twenty original paintings by some of our best artists. We sincerely hope that this [is] not to continue, but that an interest in this venture will be awakened...*

Earlier, in 1872, a painter based in Utah, George M. Ottinger, wrote:

> *In the last eight years I have painted 223 pictures which have been sold for $3415, or little more than $15 each. Now deducting $7.00 each for supplies and framing, it leaves me $1,752, or a little over half. My work is worth only $219 a year. When I look at my family and our wants I grieve...*

Renoir said: "The only reward one should offer an artist is to buy his work."[38] I think Lindstrom craved validation for his work—artists are notoriously insecure—through selling more of it. Over the many years of raising a family, Lindstrom paid the bills primarily through working as an art professor; my mother also worked full-time, first as a librarian and later as an elementary school teacher. In retirement, Lindstrom traded artwork for dental services. In the last year of his life, he told us: "I never dream about the rich, only the poor."

For his Moran lecture his primary sources were Moran's letters and journals. Lindstrom, himself, never consistently kept a journal. For most of his life, as a close adherent to his faith, the Church of Jesus Christ of Latter-Day Saints (LDS), which stresses the importance of personal histories, he did write in recollection of his youth, and he was a "pack rat." After his death we found old papers in a box upon which he had written, "No value. Discard." This prompted my mother to ask, "Why didn't he discard it?" He kept letters, postcards, emails, certificates, school grade reports, newspaper and magazine clippings, etc., loosely and in scrapbooks. I suspect he thought maybe someday, someone would write a book.

Chapter 7

Family History & Early Life

Gale William Lindstrom was born in Salt Lake City, Utah on the 4th of July, 1919. For years his children believed all the fireworks were in celebration of his birthday. His mother, Bertha, wrote that the doctor wanted them to name Lindstrom

George Washington, some wanted us to name him Jack Dempsey. One nurse at the hospital, Anna Rasmussen, said Dale was the best name for him... but he got the name of Gale, which I think is suitable, as he is swift as a gale... He weighed 9 pounds and 2 ounces. Yet the smallest ears – no bigger than a dime, but it didn't take long for them to grow. His hair was black, his face was very red, and he had big blue eyes. He never grew very fat, just long and lanky.

While still a toddler, Lindstrom would hold his breath. The first time he did this, Bertha panicked and called her mother, who quickly walked a block to catch a streetcar; twenty minutes later she got off, and then walked ten blocks to the house "to see what could be done. By the time grandmother arrived, I suppose I was breathing normally," Lindstrom wrote. As a little boy, curious about its flavor, he licked a sidewalk near his home. When asked what it tasted like, he said, "About what you'd expect." His curiosity never abated, although he gave up on sidewalks (figure 13).

Preceding Lindstrom in birth were his sisters, Helen, Lucile, and Dorothy. All three were married and out of the house when Lindstrom was still young, further cementing the place of his parents in his life. His father was William Gustav Lindstrom. Born in Sundsvall, Sweden in 1874, he was tall, with a broad face, and large ears that would become a multi-generational trademark.

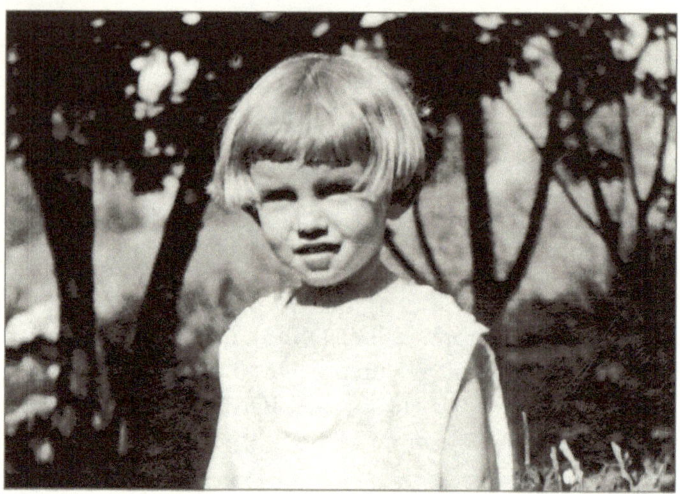

Figure 13: Gale Lindstrom, age 4

William, at age eleven, along with his mother Charlotta, sailed to the United States via Liverpool. The name "Lindstrom" was his mother's maiden name. Nothing is known about his father, other than he may have been Peter Gustav Lindgren. Mother and son arrived on Ellis Island on December 5, 1888, and would settle in Chicago. In 1898, William married for the first time, but his wife would die a year later. In the Windy City he was once accused of robbery, but was cleared mainly due to the testimony and journal entries of an LDS missionary, who was teaching the family about the church at the time.

William, at age eleven, along with Charlotta, sailed to the United States via Liverpool. The name "Lindstrom" was his mother's maiden name. Nothing is known about his father other than that he may have been Peter Gustav Lindgren. Mother and son arrived on Ellis Island on December 5, 1888, and would settle in Chicago. In 1898 William married for the first time, but his wife would die a year later. In the Windy City he was once accused of robbery, but was cleared mainly due to the testimony and journal entries of an LDS missionary, who was teaching the family about the church at the time. He was guilty, however, of shooting Roman candles into saloons while his friends held the doors open.

William would join the LDS church in 1901 and move to Salt Lake City. Lindstrom said his father spoke English without a Swedish accent and always carried a camera with him. A trained interior decorator and

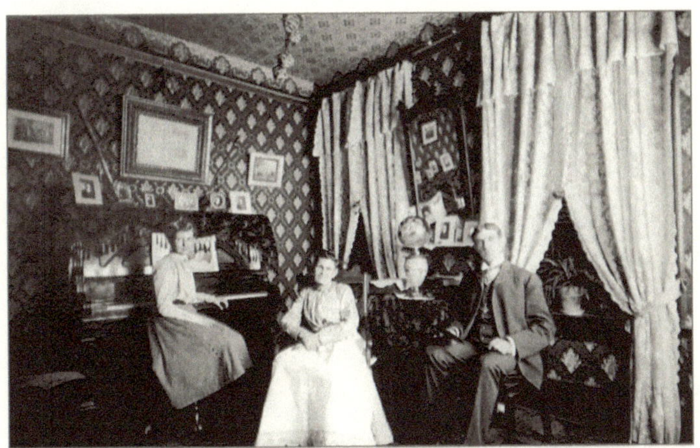

Figure 14: Hedvig, Charlotta, and William Lindstrom, Chicago apartment,

painter, he worked on private homes, LDS temples, chapels, and other church buildings throughout the Intermountain West and as far away as Palmyra, New York. He painted and did highly specialized decoration. Lindstrom remembered his father "cutting stencils at home on the dining room table" that he would then use to decorate the walls and ceilings of a chapel. "No one in the state could spread enamel better."[39] He worked for the White House, a Salt Lake City interior furnishing and decoration company, and then later owned his own business. His calling card read, "WM LINDSTROM PAINTER PAPERHANGER AND INTERIOR DECORATOR" and featured angels painting two of the letters in the job title. For the 1939 World's Fair, he traveled to San Francisco to paint and decorate a replica of Temple Square's Tabernacle on Treasure Island. He also dabbled in watercolor painting, copying illustrations from magazines.

William was a local church leader, possessed a wonderful sense of humor, and was beloved by the neighborhood boys whom he actively supported in Boy Scouts. Many years later, one of them wrote, "I can still see him putting water in the radiator of the old Hup as we were going up to Granddaddy Lakes."[40] With his fine craftsmanship and a stockpile of paint and paper he kept around the house, William undoubtedly stirred Lindstrom's interest in painting. The son would inherit from his father, in addition to the ears, a playfulness and stoicism, and a strong work ethic; the latter would chiefly manifest itself in his job as a teacher and amateur architect, builder, and landscaper.

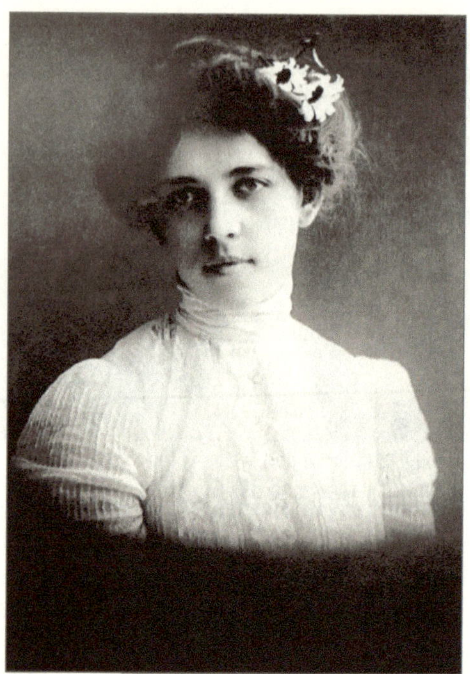

Figure 15: Bertha Thorup, Salt Lake City, circa 1907

Lindstrom's mother, Bertha Thorup (figure 15), who William affectionately called "Bert," was a wide-eyed beauty with full lips and a softly-tapered face and chin. Born to Danish immigrants in 1883 and raised in Salt Lake City, literate in Danish and English, Bertha was the first of twelve children of her polygamist father's third wife. Her grandfather, Herman A. Thorup, a trained carpenter, made the winding stairway leading to the tower of the Assembly Hall on Temple Square and the beautiful east and west doors of the Salt Lake Temple. His son and Bertha's father, Herman F.F., was a florist, who would father 19 children and serve "'Uncle Sam' for one year for 'conscience's sake.' This was a typical way to say that he spent [five months] in the State Prison because of his being married to two wives at the same time," Lindstrom wrote. Herman tended the prison gardens, grew vegetables for its kitchen, and was finally released "due to his splendid record and because of his suffering family." Along with Bertha's mother, Jensine, he endured the death of four of his children, when they were very young. In 1889, Herman was called to serve an LDS mission in Denmark. After he left, food at home became scarce. One night, during his absence, when the family had nothing in the cupboard, they knelt and prayed. Before they got off their knees, the wind blew the front door open. A child ran to close it and discovered a sack of flour. Bertha's mother wondered who brought it, so "we can thank them." Bertha said, "Mother, don't worry. If God can say, let there be light and there is light, then God can say let there be flour and there's flour." Many years later, my mother recalls Bertha carefully folding up the leftover dinner rolls at a restaurant and putting them in her purse.

Even when Bertha's father was home, money was a great concern. They lived in a two-room house next to one for Herman's other wife, Anne, and behind the family's greenhouse and store, "South Eastern Nursery," out of which Herman sold flowers, plants, shrubs, trees, and seeds. Lindstrom would stare in fascination at the water pump outside the door. "I often wondered why they poured water into the pump and then pumped it out, always seeming to get more water out than they put in." Bertha describes the flowers in bloom in the spring, a sight that would have been familiar to a young Lindstrom:

> *Such lovely violets, Lily of the Valley and forget-me-nots, lilacs and roses. Roses as big as cabbages... honeysuckle that sent its perfume everywhere. The bees and the butterflies swarmed on the heliotrope... minuet and sweet alyssum and in the fall wonderful asters. I would pick them by the armfuls and couldn't tell where I had been.*[41]

When she was just eight years old, Bertha's father took her out of school every other day to sell flowers door to door and wreaths of holly that her mother made at Christmas on Salt Lake City street corners, even in the dead of winter. Father and daughter sometimes walked all the way to Murray, nearly eight miles, to sell flowers, and then walked back. Later, Bertha washed other people's clothes and, beginning at the age of 14, dipped chocolates at J. G. McDonald Chocolate Company for $3 a week. After she married, Bertha worked at the Remington arms plant during World War II and operated a chocolate business out of her home. Still, her own family struggled financially. One Christmas Lindstrom got a new coat of paint on his sled. "I think my Dad thought I might not recognize the sled and think it was a new one." Worried about her children and not wanting them to suffer as she had, Bertha sent all of them to a business college after high school. If they could type and take shorthand, they could get a job. She was concerned when

Lindstrom announced he wanted to be artist. "I didn't receive much encouragement from my parents. My mother thought artists starved and I don't think my dad gave it much thought."

Lindstrom always spoke highly of his parents, especially his mother. On the European tours he helped lead, some of which lasted up to eight weeks, he sent her postcards from virtually every stop. She was her only son's mentor in "lots of things." She provided him with musical instruments and paid ten dollars down and four dollars a month for ten months, for a used French horn at Daynes Music Company. It took her ten months to pay the balance. She also paid for piano and art lessons and his tuition at the business college and later the University of Utah. Lindstrom studied piano with Frederic Dixon, a University of Utah professor who had played with major U.S. symphonies. They became good friends, and Lindstrom worked as Dixon's chauffeur. Lindstrom's parents also provided him with a small art studio, attached to the family house (figure 16).

Into her 80s, Bertha worked as a laundress at the Hotel Utah beginning every day at 6am. After work she would walk two blocks to the city library where she took art classes, then boarded a trolley car for home. When she couldn't work any longer, she moved to Logan, while Lindstrom was teaching at USU, and lived in a nursing home. Sally Scholes, a nurse who took care of Bertha, said, "Nobody had a child that visited them every day. But your father came every day to see his mother."

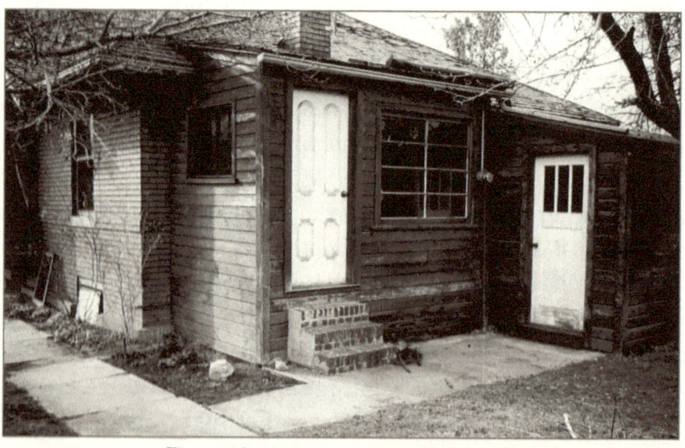

Figure 16: Lindstrom's first studio, entrance on the right

Although his father always had paint around the house, and his sister Helen, who tried her hand at oil painting, once gave him a 60 cent set of watercolor paints, Lindstrom may never have developed into the artist he became without the influence of his mother. She exemplified humility, grace, a love of beauty, and proper manners, and passed these on to her only son.

Chapter 8

School & The Young Artist

It's been said of Picasso that, when painting, "his eyes widen, his nostrils flare, he frowns, he attacks the canvas like a picador sticking a bull."[42] This image may have horrified Bertha. In contrast, Lindstrom would sit on a chair with two seat cushions, turn his head from side to side, squint, and then make a stroke like a conductor directing the first delicate notes of Beethoven's *Ninth*. The cool clinician. But like Atticus Finch, the outward appearance masked an internal conflict. He wrote in an artist's statement: "A large, blank, white sheet of watercolor paper is a frightening spectacle. I never feel comfortable while painting; excited at times, but never at ease nor quite ahead of the medium." There is a wildness to the medium of watercolor and in Lindstrom's skies and Chinese-inspired paintings, he didn't try to tame it.

What Picasso said of himself, I believe is true of Lindstrom: "I paint the way some people write their autobiography. The paintings, finished or not, are the pages of my journal...."[43] This explains, at least in part, why Lindstrom never consistently kept a diary. He didn't need to. Renoir said about Paul Cezanne: "We have his pictures, which tell us more about him than the very best biographer could ever do."[44] Still, one wishes that Lindstrom, like his idol van Gogh, would have drawn a self-portrait or two, to allow us the opportunity to tease out more of what he saw in himself.

In regard to his artistic development, he was fortunate, in many ways, to have been born in Salt Lake City. Taught by LDS missionaries, European and American converts answered the call to come to Utah and build up "Zion." Included in their ranks were many artists, who themselves would mentor aspiring Utah-born artists, encouraging them to study in Paris or New York. This included Lindstrom's future art teachers—J.T. Harwood, Lee Greene Richards, Joseph A.F. Everett, and LeConte Stewart. The list of Utah painters would eventually grow long and distinguished. What also attracted artists to the state is its world-class landscapes. Albert Bierstadt first visited the state in 1863 and Thomas Moran in 1873.

Although Utahns were and remain conservative in purchasing art, these artists and others did foster the population's interest in and celebration of the arts. Brigham Young and his band of Latter-Day Saints had arrived in 1847. Young said if he was stranded on an island and charged with civilizing the natives, the first thing he would do is build a theater.[45] And so he did. By 1850, outdoor theater performances were entertaining the saints. Dedicated in 1853, the Social Hall shielded playgoers from the elements. The Salt Lake Theatre, which presented plays, operas, ballets, dances, magicians, and musclemen, would follow in 1862, pre-dating the opening of the Salt Lake LDS temple by thirty-one years. Theaters were not just places for civilizing. An early Salt Lake actress remarked, "We were far away from everywhere, cut off from the world, with nothing but the faults and foibles of our neighbors to amuse us."[46] Even today LDS churches are equipped with pulpits and theater stages. Early settlers also founded the University of Deseret in 1850 to teach art, literature, and philosophy,[47] and established in 1899 the Utah Arts Institute, the first arts agency in the United States.

Today there are theaters and art organizations throughout the state, even in the smallest towns. One percent of all public capital projects in cities from Ogden to Saint George are set aside for public art. According to a 2015 National Endowment for the Arts report, Utahns ranked first in attending a visual or performing arts event, art exhibit, or watching a film.[48] The state boasts a world-class film festival, Sundance, and the Tony Award-winning Utah Shakespeare Festival. In Salt Lake City the Devereaux House, Governor's Mansion, and the LDS temple are architectural gems. Lindstrom exhibited his work in shows held in museums, the state capitol building, an LDS institute of religion, a department store, a furniture store, and the Utah Power and Light Company's auditorium.

The world of his childhood was a banquet for the senses, certainly a treat for a boy with an insatiable curiosity. Northwest of the Lindstrom family house, on 2539 South and 13th East, was downtown Salt Lake City, and to the south, rural farmland—unpaved roads, a stream, alfalfa pastures, and livestock. In a picture of his third-grade class, Lindstrom wears a bow tie and long-sleeved sweater, while several of his male classmates wear short-sleeved shirts and farmer's overalls. He recalled his youth for an essay in a first-year writing course at the University of Utah. He and his friends would push their

> *tiny wagons to the old Country Club hollow, loading them with hay, and then leaving most of it strewn on the paths which led home to our waiting rabbits. An excursion of this sort meant not just cutting the fresh, green lucerne, but also a dip in the old seventh hole dam, which was conveniently lined with numerous willow growths and wild roses which made it at least semi-private for our nude bodies.*

On one occasion, he tumbled down a hill, hitting his arm against the wagon, and opening up a three-inch gash on his arm, exposing a "gleaming, chalk white, bone." However, his concern for the rabbits outweighed other considerations, so he tied a dirty handkerchief "around the wound and began cutting the load for the day." When he got home his mother fainted and his father rushed him to the doctor.

Across the street from the Lindstrom's was the "Highland Home," a small building for LDS meetings and Friday night silent movies. In charge of the congregation's Amusement Committee, William (his official title was "Stage Manager") operated the projector and showed a new movie every Friday night. One of Lindstrom's music teachers, Miriam Bishop, accompanied the silent films on the piano. William also performed as a magician—he made large white jars float at his command and sawed his daughter in half. One year, along with a colleague, he "put together a tent large enough to house a 'three-ring circus.' The 'animals' were... animated by ward members, it sometimes taking as many [as] four men to animate one 'animal.'"[49] Replacing the Highland Home in 1925 was a Tudor Revival meeting house that William helped build. On the inside the chapel and amusement hall were of a Gothic design with a high pointed ceiling and the walls and ceiling in the chapel were finished with a coarsely raked stucco. John Fairbanks, the father of Avard, who would become a nationally-known sculptor, decorated the entry way with two murals of pioneers, one showing them crossing the plains in covered wagons and the other depicting a wintery scene in which some of the pioneers in the Salt Lake valley were housed in log cabins while others braved the cold in wagons and tents.

Inside, Lee Greene Richards' impressionistic paintings of Biblical sites including the Sea of Galilee and the Mount of Olives decorated the four corners of the chapel, each embedded inside a Gothic niche. Behind the pupil was his large mural of the Sacred Grove, where Latter-Day Saints believe Joseph Smith saw God the Father and Jesus Christ in upstate New York. Behind the chapel, the amusement hall was lit by ornamental wall sconces. As a child, Lindstrom spent a great deal of time here attending socials and church meetings. In 2000, he said it was "still one of the finest of all LDS church buildings." Screenings of silent movies would continue in the amusement hall with Lindstrom's best friend, Hugh C. Brown, operating the projector. "When a bucolic scene appeared on the screen, he would slip a green plate of glass in front of the lens. When... a fire or a sunset appeared, a red glass would be slipped in front of the lens."

Down the street and around the corner from the chapel lived the Maack family. George, the father, smoked large cigars and worked as a sign painter and artist. He painted the large curtain for Salt Lake's Pantages Theater. Completed in 1918, complete with a Tiffany skylight, the neoclassical vaudeville palace could seat 2200 patrons and featured a variety of acts from Babe Ruth to Will Rogers to Abbott and Costello before becoming a movie theater. Always well-lit, its curtain stayed in place before performances and screenings, "so everyone could read about 50 different advertisements, displayed in a most artistic manner by Mr. Maack," according to Lindstrom. Atop his garage at home, Mr. Maack constructed an observatory that boasted a movable dome and a giant telescope. He frequently invited the neighborhood kids over for "an evening's entertainment" observing the stars.

Not far away from the family home and church, Lindstrom's grandmother, Charlotta, lived in a small, yellow house with no running water. Lindstrom remembered the white and red plaid kitchen, a "table cloth of Italian design," his grandmother's yellow pound cakes "not much larger than a solid pound of butter," the "Danish pudding"—rigrut, red mush, with fresh raspberries that "complemented the pound cake in every way including color," "the tinkling Japanese glass chimes which hung outside," and the wooden sidewalk in the summer covered with "dark purple stains from a mulberry tree." Lindstrom didn't remember much about Charlotta herself, other than her "heavy gold earrings [and] gold teeth, which were a bit intimidating, her old-fashioned high collar dresses. I can still see the red-globed *Gone With the Wind*-style kerosene lamp that graced a table in her small living room."

Thinking a warmer climate would be good for her health, Bertha would take a young Lindstrom on two trips to southern California, the longest six weeks. They traveled to Catalina Island on a glass-bottomed boat and visited friends from Los Angeles to San Francisco. While back in Los Angeles, they felt the effects of the 1925 Santa Barbara earthquake. Bertha wrote: "Our beds rocked and dishes rattled so we thought we had better go home." I can imagine the impression this made on the six-year-old Lindstrom. He returned often to California (figure 17), discovering in San Francisco at age 14 the work of Diego Rivera, who became his favorite Mexican artist. In one of Lindstrom's scrapbooks, I found a carefully preserved photograph of Rivera's famous mural, *The Making of a Fresco Showing the Building of a City.*

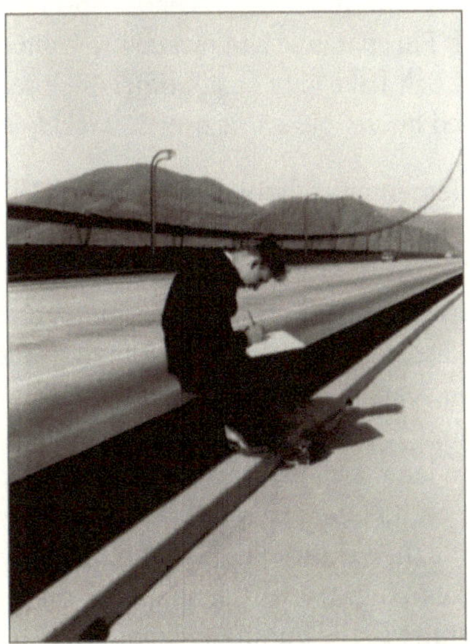

Figure 17: Lindstrom sketching on the Golden Gate Bridge,

Lindstrom's formal education began in Mary Robinson's first-grade class at Highland Park School, a seven-block walk from home. At the time, George N. Child, Superintendent of Salt Lake City Public Schools, reminded parents and pupils that with "right living, proper health habits and proper attention to physical condition, HEALTH is attained and disease prevented. Remember HEALTH cannot be bought."[50] The school district required parents twice a year to submit a "Health and Weight Record" for each of their children. Lindstrom would spend two years with Mary Robinson. "I was ill so much of my first year that I was asked to stay an extra year …she told me that very plainly and I said nothing but was quite disappointed." Indeed, poor health real or imagined was a cause of concern throughout Lindstrom's life. As an adult, he cut short a trip to Puerto Rico and stopped painting if he wasn't feeling well.

Based on multiple accounts, Bertha coddled her youngest when he was a child. On his first overnight Boy Scout experience, one that would require a four-mile hike, she loaded him "with eight quilts, two suitcases, a tent, and plenty of first aid equipment... I looked like a procession of bundles moving by some magic force." But this coddling should be looked at in light of the times. Bertha's father didn't believe in doctors and her mother-in-law had lost two children to diphtheria. Typhoid and polio were serious realities, and a Spanish Flu epidemic had racked the United States a year before Lindstrom's birth. Salt Lake City health officials closed schools and put in quarantine infected households. Still, over 500 residents died.

Lindstrom's elementary school report cards listed grades in the three "R's" and "Health Habits." In his second year with Miss Robinson, Lindstrom earned a "C" in Health Habits the first grading period and an "A" in the last. It appears illness was a recurring problem: of the 39 days of school in the last marking period of fourth grade, he was absent 26 times. But the two years in first grade were actually a boon for the future artist. With toothpicks, Miss Robinson's students created the letters of the alphabet, then later spelled "words with small square pieces of paper each with a letter on it." One day, on the blackboard, she drew an outline of a pumpkin. "She then showed us 'how' to fill in the outline. She made quite a few strokes contrary to the shape of the pumpkin and made strokes in conformity to the pumpkin's contours. The latter was the 'way to go.'" Lindstrom never forgot this and to the end of his days, he said he could still see Miss Robinson at that chalkboard with that pumpkin. She must have been a demanding art teacher: Lindstrom earned "B's" in drawing in second grade, but in third grade, with a different teacher, Deane Maddison, his average grade was an "A."

"In the fourth grade Ione Naegle taught us much about the arts and I guess my interest in such was really developed at this time," Lindstrom wrote. By the fifth grade, specialists taught each subject, including art. "We had a music class and an art class [taught by Miss Baders] every day."

The teachers were strict, but once the kids got to the soccer field the rules went out the window. Lindstrom recalls, "One could kick the ball, throw the ball, run with the ball, or simply ignore the ball and fight with someone from the other side. It was… a much more interesting game than the way soccer is played today."

At Highland Park he would meet Hugh C. Brown, son of Hugh B. Brown, a member of the Quorum of the Twelve Apostles and First Presidency of the Church of Jesus Christ of Latter-Day Saints. The elder Brown was a major in the Canadian military, a lawyer, professor, life-long Democrat, and Lindstrom's stake president, an ecclesiastical leader. Hugh C. bloodied Lindstrom's nose. From then on they were best friends. In 1938, while serving a church mission in London, Hugh wrote his boyhood pal, whom he called "Lindsty." "I have certainly thought a lot about all the good times that we have had together... Breaking Arc-lights, playing football, climbing in trees, spring, photography, hamburgers, and at last [sic], our girlfriends."[51] Hugh attended the rival South High School, but one day he happened to appear at the door of Lindstrom's classroom at East High. He handed the teacher a note and left. As Clayton Robbins, another friend, recalled, "the teacher announced that Gaell Lindstrom was to report to the office. These two wayward youth were turned loose on the world and who knows what mischief resulted."[52] During World War II, Hugh volunteered for the Royal Air Force. He was killed while on a submarine reconnaissance mission over the English Channel in 1942. For over sixty years, Lindstrom kept a newspaper article announcing Hugh's death and praising his heroism. The loss of Hugh while in the prime of his life contributed to Lindstrom's abhorrence of war.

During the Great Depression, when Lindstrom was 12 years old, he purchased his first camera, a Univex, from the Schramm-Johnson drugstore for 25 cents. From that time on, like his father, he always had a camera with him. Film cost 10 cents and processing another 10 cents. "So, basically $.35 started my career as a photographer." This was the time of his initiation into the Boy Scouts. Lindstrom and other scouts annually hiked two miles above Mirror Lake with all their gear to Camp Steiner. At 10,400 feet it is still the highest scout camp in the United States. Lindstrom recalled:

The mountains were something to be reckoned with. The most beautiful was Hayden Peak rising over 13,000 feet... Two other favorites were Mount Baldy and Reids Peak, one flat topped and the other a high pointed arrowhead kind of mountain. On my last trip to the Uintas, I took pictures with my first camera... [it] made pictures the size of a 35mm slide.

That same year, he would complete a small watercolor of a mountain and lake (figure 18). The painting demonstrated some budding talent in color and composition, and his interest in mountains.

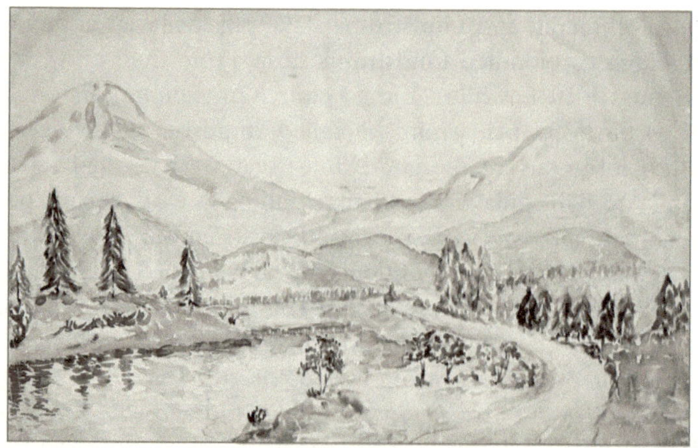

Figure 18: Lindstrom watercolor, circa 1932

At Irving Junior High School, a late Victorian-style building decorated with enough finials to impale a flock of pigeons, Bob Snow, an older boy who designed model airplanes with Lindstrom, encouraged his younger friend to take a mechanical drawing class. Lindstrom was doing well in the class, but one day the principal told him it "was only for 9th graders and had me withdraw. I remember walking after him down the hall with tears in my eyes. But, who was someone just out of the 7th grade to argue with a man as big as Mr. Hagen? I look at this incident as wiping out my beginning career as an architect."

Lindstrom developed a photographic memory, but this didn't always translate into good school grades. In his first year at Irving, he earned a D average in English, C in Latin, and B in Art. The results were similar the following year. He had two art classes a day from Verla Birrell, a "good watercolor painter" and an "excellent teacher." Lindstrom never forgot her, inviting her to his 1986 retrospective. In class they used mostly watercolor paint because of her interests and the expense of oils. He wrote:

> *I think I learned almost all of what I know in her class. The ninth grade she had a special art class which I was invited to become a member. It was in this class that I did my first oil painting. I had managed to get enough oil paint together from my father's tubes of tinting colors to do the small painting (figure 19), which was hung high on one of the blackboards in the art room. I think most of what I know about composition and about perspective I learned in her class. I learned about light and dark... how to mix paint. This, as well as the many ways of using watercolor.*

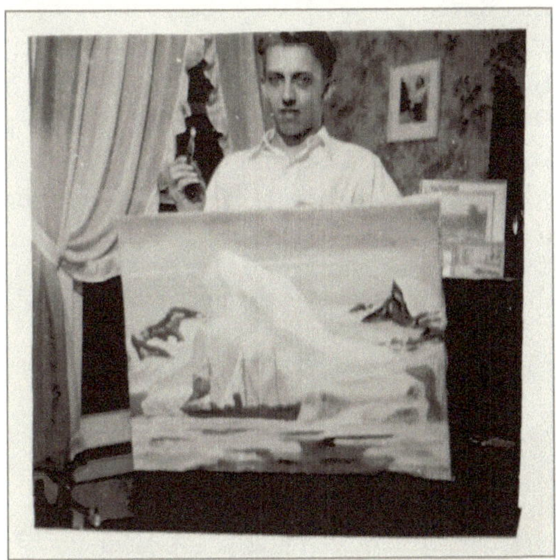

Figure 19: Lindstrom, age 14 in Salt Lake City

He would often ask for more watercolor paint, especially purple, "a great color." Lindstrom also liked to paint in black. "I used to get big pieces of newspaper and hang them up on the side of the garage. I could always find a bucket of paint somewhere, and I remember painting up these pieces of ... paper, copying Rodin's *The Thinker*." This early interest in the color black foreshadows his work in the 1960s in charcoal, and later his interest in Chinese painting. Birrell's course included other arts, including working with leather. Lindstrom created an art deco design for a leather wallet.

Lindstrom was too young to fully understand the upheavals of the Great Depression. He did recall that his mother, whenever someone came calling to the house, "could put a meal together within minutes. When I could see little in the kitchen in the way of food." He bene-fited from President Roosevelt's New Deal. The Works Progress Admin-istration (WPA) employed many local artists as teachers at Salt Lake City's art center. Lindstrom regularly visited the center and received free lessons. Roosevelt's programs also employed artists to create thousands of public pieces, including the murals that decorate the interior of the Utah state capitol's dome depicting romanticized images of, for example, mountain men, LDS pioneers, Catholic missionaries, Brigham Young declaring, "This is the place!", and seagulls that saved early settlers' crops from crickets. Along with the local community, the WPA constructed a Spanish Colonial Revival-style building that became the Springville Art Museum. Dedicated by LDS church apostle David O. McKay as "a sanc-tuary of beauty and a temple of meditation,"[53] it annually hosts a Spring Salon, which often featured Lindstrom's work. The tangible benefits of the WPA and other New Deal programs Lindstrom and others he knew benefited from, fed what would become his long-held belief that government can help people.

For his 16th birthday, Bertha gave him a small card which read:

Good for 10 art lessons
from Mr. J.T. Harwood
1718 Lake St
Commencing Friday morning July-5.

A former art department chair at the University of Utah, James Taylor Harwood was the first native Utah artist to study in Paris. At the time, many of the great French impressionists were doing some of their best work. Harwood attended the Académie Julian and was the first Utahn to exhibit his work at the Paris Salon. In the program that accompanied a 1940 retrospective, the artist's daughter, Ruth Harwood, wrote: "He was born in Lehi, and as a school boy felt the urge to express in beauty."[54] Lindstrom recalled their time together:

Across the street from Mr. Harwood's studio was a neighbor's house with hollyhocks in full bloom and all was back-lighted with the early summer sun – perfect subjects for an impressionistic painting. I followed Mr. Harwood's approach and made a preliminary pastel sketch on tinted paper (figure 20) before attempting a painting. During one lesson I was shown some of his pastel sketches of French and Italian subjects. Actually, very little of the scenes were represented, mostly just high-lights. I asked him how he was able to make such large paintings from such little information. He said that I should remember that he had painted out-of-doors for many years, which experience enabled him to fill in the empty parts of the sketch. Mr. Harwood seemed pleased with the work I completed and mentioned that he thought I had "caught on" rather quickly.

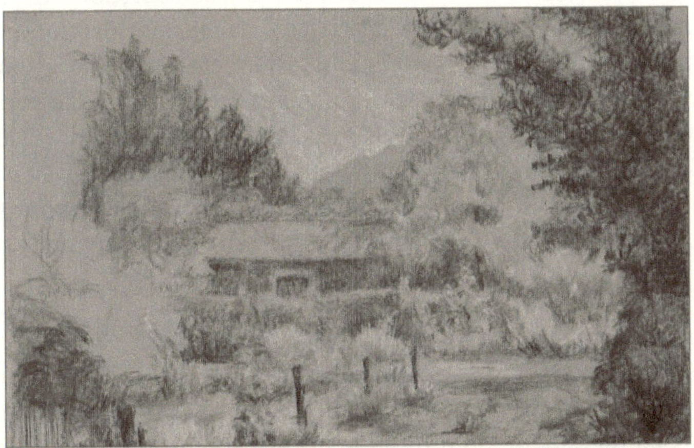

Figure 20: Lindstrom pastel drawing, 1935 (as a student of J.T. Harwood)

After attending West High School for a week, Lindstrom decided it was too far away from home, and, as South High was new but had "no character," Lindstrom settled on attending East High, although it was an 18 block walk, the last two up a steep hill. While a single streetcar ride was cheap, one had to buy 50 tickets at a time for a hard-to-earn $2. On occasion he had the luxury of riding in the back of a friend's Model T Ford, which would start as it coasted down a driveway. For "super luxury," his father sometimes allowed him to drive the family's 1926 Hupmobile which, unlike the Ford, had doors and windows. At that time one could buy an automobile for $500. Lindstrom appreciated good design in everything from cars to fireplaces to buildings, although he would never own a car as elegant as a Hupp with its spoked wheels, whitewall tires, curved running board, fish-gill vents, winged "H" hood ornament, and bug-eyed headlights. I'm sure the tall, teenage, and now Errol Flynn-looking Lindstrom in a "sport coat, two-tone shirt and tie" must have cut quite a picture as he stepped out of the Hupp in the East High parking lot. Unfortunately, Lindstrom forgot to change the oil in the car and burned out its bearings; his father sold it for $50.

For entertainment Lindstrom and friends took a trolley and then a train along a causeway in the Great Salt Lake to a stately G-rated pleasure-dome named "Saltair." Opened in 1893 and built atop 2000 pylons hammered into the lake bed, with its lacy wood trim and onion domes, it was envisioned as the "Coney Island of the West." Designed by Richard K.A. Kletting, the architect of the Utah state capitol building, it sported a roller coaster, Ferris Wheel, hot dog stands, shooting gallery, Ali Baba's Cave, a Hippodrome, and a large dance floor that looked out over the lake and its "Waikiki Beach." The main reason to go was to lie in the salt water, where pleasure-seekers could bob "like corks in the briny Great Salt Lake."[55] At its peak, the playground drew 500,000 people a year. Glenn Miller and the other big bands of the day played at Saltair. Lindstrom wrote: "I remember being in the ballroom some evenings and watching the lightning from across the lake [and] at the same time inhaling the... strong salty air."

Lindstrom grew up in an era when high school students could major in a subject(s). He graduated from East in 1937 with a major in art and music, playing in the orchestra and ROTC band. Thinking like his mother about job prospects, he wrote, "I should've majored in mechanical drawing and architectural design and did well... with Mary Maine, a great teacher." Apparently this interest wasn't totally squashed in junior high school, and accounts in part for his eye for painting composition. However, most of his fellow students who signed his high school yearbook, single out not his drawing but music: "...I hope you will become another famous Bach at writing and at playing the piano," "Here's to a good alto man," and, "You may blow some blue notes now and then but your [sic] still okay." He played the French horn along with Benny Winn and the two became close friends. Their senior year of high school they took a road trip to southeast Utah, Lindstrom's first visit to "super spectacular" Dead Horse Point. Despite a burned out generator, the boys managed to drive all the way back to Salt Lake City. The trip to

"God's country," as he would come to call it, further whetted his appetite to see more of the world and its visual spendors.

In high school he would often stay after school in the art room and draw the Greek and Roman sculptures it housed, life-size replicas of famous works.

One night, along with his friend Clayton Robbins, he stayed late, only to learn that they were locked inside the school. In vain they looked for a way out. Robbins remembered that "in the process of exploring the kitchen we discovered a stack of freshly baked pie shells." Lindstrom was "intrigued to find they had similar flight characteristics to a frisbee."[56] What follows doesn't take much imagination. On another occasion, the pair drove William's car out to Black Rock, on the Great Salt Lake, to spend a day at the beach, but it was a cold and windy day. They sat "in the car drinking pop, when suddenly an empty shattered the driver's side window [Lindstrom]… slamming an empty pop bottle through it—thinking it had been rolled down."[57] Robbins wondered how Lindstrom would explain what happened to his father.

After high school he played the French horn for several area orchestras including the Salt Lake City Opera Association, which performed *Faust, Babette, Gondoliers,* and *The New Moon.* In performance programs he's variously listed as "Gaell," "Gayle," and "Gale Lynstrom."[58] He would eventually adopt and sign his paintings "Gaell." Upon the creation of the Utah Symphony in 1940, he quit playing, although he would attend practically all of their performances for several years in the famous domed Salt Lake Tabernacle with its enormous roof, world-class acoustics, and pine wood benches and pillars, the latter "marbleized by European convert artisans."[59] One critic described the tabernacle as "a prodigious tortoise that has lost its way," while Frank Lloyd Wright called it "one of the architectural masterpieces of the country and perhaps the world."[60]

Lindstrom's study at business college included math, shorthand, typing, bookkeeping, and penmanship. Occasionally the college would send him out on odd jobs: addressing envelopes with letters to prospective stock investors—he could type 150 addresses an hour—for Mr. A.B. Thomas "who constantly smoked long cigars." As a First National Bank messenger, he was paid $750 a year based on a 42-hour work week. Once a month employees worked late to complete customer statements.

The bank would then treat their employees to dinner; Lindstrom always ordered the prime rib for 55 cents, including a drink and dessert. He sometimes dared to order ice cream at five cents a scoop extra, but the bank never complained.

Chapter 9

Missionary Adventures

In October of 1940 Lindstrom was called as an LDS missionary to serve in the East Central States Mission. Before leaving he would record his ambitions: "1. To be an accomplished artist, 2. To be an accomplished pianist, and 3. To have some desirable female companion." At a farewell party in his boyhood home, his friends drew pictures of Lindstrom on 9 x 12 sheets of brown paper depicting him as a painter at his easel, while in others he's seated at a piano. In one, labeled "Professor Lindstrom," he's the mad pianist, limbs flailing. One of the most striking drawings (figure 21) demonstrates the general attitude in Salt Lake City about modern art.

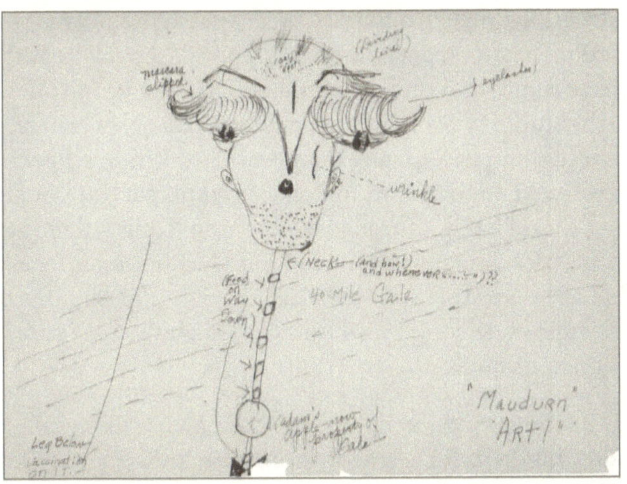

Figure 21: Drawing by Lindstrom's friend at farewell party, 1940

While training at the Salt Lake Mission Home, he wrote of himself and other green missionaries: "We are all curious but not concerned with where we will be sent when we reach our headquarters at Louisville. It may be anywhere in Kentucky, West Virginia, Virginia, Tennessee, or North Carolina. It would certainly be fine to be stationed in some Atlantic Coast fishing village." He departed for the East in January, 1941. Stopping in Nashville, Lindstrom and his fellow greenhorns visited Forest Park and "the magnificent art galleries and the zoo and other buildings. The art museum is the finest I have ever seen. It has the actual rooms of Louis XV and also the furniture made into rooms in the museum. It also has marvelous pieces of sculpture and collections of French miniatures." Once he reached Kentucky, reality hit. While serving in a damp, cold Louisville he wrote home to say the weather in Arizona would be more to his liking. His Salt Lake City Bishop, Clarence Tingey, replied with a story of a Dutch physician who wrote a book titled, *The Secret of My Medical Success*. All the pages were blank except one, which read: "Keep your head cool and your feet warm."[61] This advice was either ignored or didn't work because, after serving for three months in Louisville and becoming ill, Lindstrom was sent home to rest for 16 months. During this time he worked as a stenographer and cost clerk for Broderick & Gordon, general contractors who built manufacturing plants for the war effort.

Upon his return to the mission he was assigned to Beckley, West Virginia where he met two women who operated Stallards, a photography studio. They took portrait photographs of the missionary (figure 22) and later taught him more about photo processing and allowed him access to the studio to print his own photographs. "I, of course, became more interested in photography than ever." For WJLS, a Beckley radio station, he played on the piano, live on air, hymns such as "Gently Raise the Sacred Strain" and "Through Deepening Trails," then at church he might play Rachmaninoff's Prelude in C Minor and Tchaikovsky's Piano Concerto No. 1. He wrote in his journal: "I'm afraid people out here don't appreciate good music and consequently don't care whether I play for them or not."

While hitching rides, pedaling bicycles, and walking all over the rural South, Lindstrom became acquainted with the poor. One of his companions, Elder Taylor, would tell him of an experience stopping at an unfamiliar house when a family was having dinner. The matron of the home asked him if he had had supper. When he said no, she promptly sat him down and took some food from her family's plates and gave it to Taylor. Lindstrom would have similar experiences: "About 7pm we came to a house and the owner, after explaining our message,

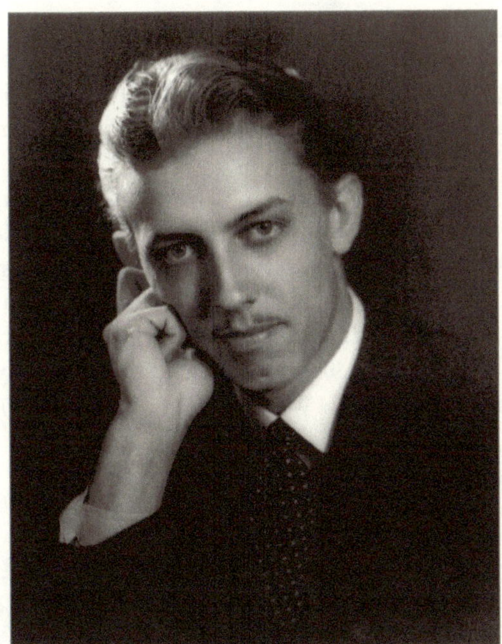

Figure 22: Lindstrom, Beckley, West Virginia, 1942

offered us money, which we of course rejected. He then told us he would give us a bed for the night but if he did he would have to sleep in the chicken coop..." At another place down the hill, the missionaries were "cordially ushered in by [a farmer's] snuff chewing wife who insisted on preparing lunch for us. They were very poor people..." One family only had three eggs to feed themselves and the missionaries, while a hotel manager, when Lindstrom asked "what the preacher price was," offered to let the missionaries stay the night for free. Because of his keen awareness of the struggles of his mother, he felt a kinship with the poor in the South, who were always generous. His mission, I believe, helped him develop an empathy that informed his art.

After being transferred to Virginia, according to the *Radford News Journal*, Lindstrom spoke to the Radford Rotary Club at the Governor Tyler Hotel, "presenting a talk and pictures in technicolor of the Grand Canyon in Colorado. Lindstrom gave a very interesting talk and the lecture and pictures were well received by the members of the club."[62] He also made the art section of a West Virginia newspaper regarding his drawing in an "Art in Religion" exhibit at the Huntington Arts Center.

In an April 1943 letter to his parents, Lindstrom mentions his missionary companion's coat was sent by mistake to Washington, D.C., which precipitated a trip to the nation's capital. "We were very lucky in that it was cherry blossom time and never have I seen such a beautiful sight!" He also wrote that by the look of things in the capital one would never have known there was a war going on. In one breathless sentence, he writes about sitting in on Congressional sessions and going "all through the capitol and library of congress and the supreme court building and the Mellon Art Galleries and Smithsonian Institute and Lincoln Memorial and still didn't see it all." He then mentions that his music lessons "will cost 3.50 per week including harmony from a fairly decent teacher," and that he watched *Gone with the Wind* for a third time.

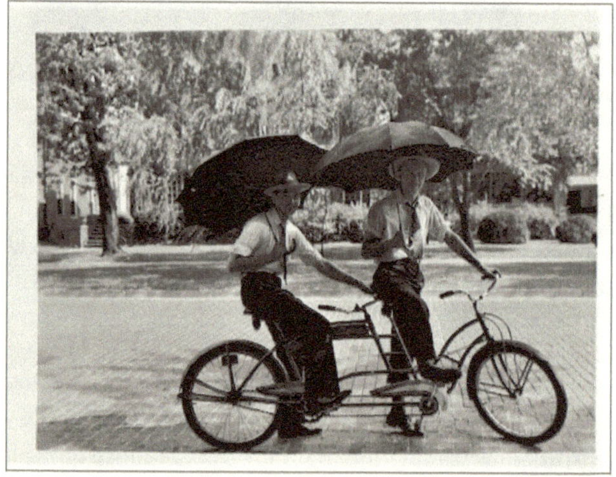

Figure 23: Elders Grant Fredickson and Gaell Lindstrom Huntington, West Virginia summer 1942

A talk on the Grand Canyon, exhibiting one's artwork, traveling to a cherry blossom festival outside one's mission boundaries, taking music lessons, and watching Clark Gable tell Vivien Leigh he didn't give a damn, would not be considered typical missionary activities today; it certainly wasn't on my mission to Washington state. However, at this time the LDS church in the South was little known, the only congregations were a few small branches scattered around five states, any positive publicity couldn't hurt, and missionary morale, considering the low conversion rates, was especially important.

During Sunday services missionaries were called upon to do just about everything. Lindstrom once played a piano duet with the mission president's daughter for the Louisville Branch Primary (for children under the age of 12). In all he would spend 27 months in the Southeast, eventually serving as the editor, printer, and artist for the *Courier*, the East Central States Mission news magazine. Graham H. Doxey, his last mission president, wrote to him about the magazine: "I think we have had the finest, most skillful workmanship that I have seen. You are a man of many talents, with art, music, and a lot of fine things."[63]

What would also be unusual today, and is representative of Lindstrom's trademark curiosity, are his letters to a church apostle. He wrote to John A. Widstoe, Harvard-educated, university president, author of books and articles on theology, and editor of the church magazine the *Improvement Era*. Lindstrom inquired about the authenticity of the

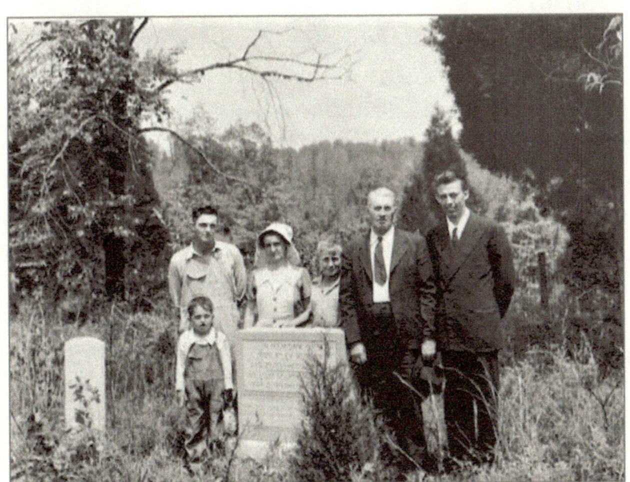

Figure 24: Elders Riego Hawkins and Gaell Lindstrom w Talley Family at Elders Gibbs and Berry gravesite Cane Creek Tenn May 1944

"Epistle of Kallikrates," published in a 1928 issue of the *Atlantic Monthly*, purporting to be a letter from the Apostle Paul to Kallikrates, a cultured man and member of the early Christian church in Corinth on the subject of the baptism of the dead. Widstoe wrote to Lindstrom that the letter is not authentic and concludes with, "I am glad you are thinking about these important matters."[64]

At the suggestion of church president Heber J. Grant, Lindstrom was released in May, 1944. He returned to Salt Lake City by train toting a Civil War sword—a birthday present—and a double-barreled, breech-loading shotgun. Sixty years earlier, in what would be called the Cane Creek Massacre, two LDS missionaries, along with step brothers who attempted to protect them from a gun-wielding mob, were gunned down in Tennessee. Before one of the brothers was shot, he killed the mob's leader with this shotgun (figure 24). Not long after, Brigham H. Roberts, then serving in the Southern States Mission, dressed as a tramp to retrieve the missionaries' bodies and sent them back to their families in Utah Territory. On their visit in May, 1944, Lindstrom and his companion asked the brothers' family, still in possession of the shotgun, if they would donate it to the church's history museum. They agreed.[65]

World War II would not end until late 1945. Lindstrom reported to the draft board but was never called to active duty. The same day he visited the Salt Lake unemployment office asking about photography jobs, a man named Ellis Park was upstairs in search of a darkroom technician. Lindstrom, thanks to the women who taught him in Beckley, West Virginia, went to work at Park's studio—his first professional photography job. He would work at two other photography studios until he opened his own, along with Gael Boden, located in the Continental Bank building in downtown Salt Lake City. It was aptly named "Gaels: Artists and Photographers." Much of the equipment Lindstrom used he had accumulated over the years since buying his first camera. They "did all kinds of photography, portraits, or commercial work or whatever people demanded." He struggled but managed to complete a commission to photograph Orson Wells, in town to perform *Othello*. Apparently, the actor had been drinking.

Chapter 10

OFF TO COLLEGE

After almost two years of operating the studio, Lindstrom decided to go back to school in 1947, this time at the University of Utah, at the age of 27. He was particularly interested in studying painting with LeConte Stewart, who was then the head of the art department. He wrote: "I didn't think about a degree or anything like that. I just wanted to learn something from LeConte Stewart." Born and raised in Utah, Stewart studied at the Art Students League in New York. A realist and primarily an oil painter, he helped create murals for the LDS church's Hawai'i and Cardston, Canada temples and would later become known as the "godfather of Utah landscape."[66] Lindstrom, who would enjoy a long association with Stewart, once told me his mentor would gaze at the Grand Tetons, then turn his back on them and paint what stood opposite. Stewart wouldn't try to improve upon God's greatest creations. "Pretty hard to do that," Lindstrom said.

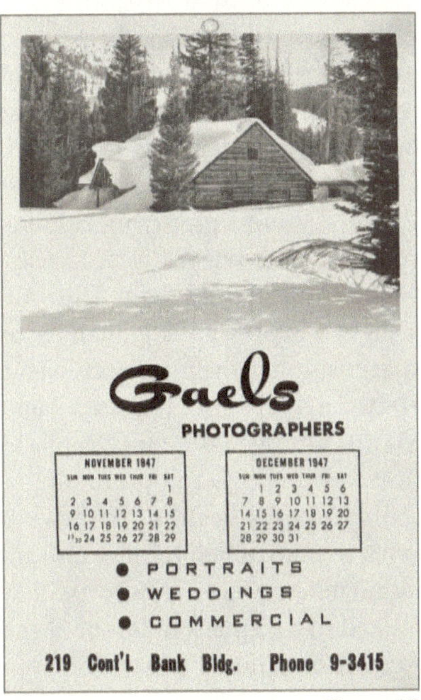

Figure 25

That same year, 1947, Lindstrom displayed his work for the first time, in a statewide show: the Utah State Institute of Fine Arts annual exhibition at the state capitol building. The following year, in the senior amateur division at the Utah State Fair, he would earn the first award for his work: an honorable mention for a painting titled *Red Barn*.

Lindstrom's father died in January 1949. Lindstrom was not quite 30. His boyhood friend Bill Richards sent his condolences from California, where he was studying music at UC Berkeley, and added a note of encouragement:

> *Your dad had good reason to be proud of you, Gaell, for you possess [his] same qualities of humility, faithfulness and kindness that endeared him to so many. These fine qualities, which are distinctively "Lindstrom qualities," together with your splendid mind and artistic ability, will assure you of a rich, happy and useful life.*[67]

In June of 1949, LeConte Stewart and Avard Fairbanks, dean of the College of Fine Arts, awarded Lindstrom "special distinction for your work entered in the Student Spring Art Exhibit... *Landscape*, represents superior craftsmanship in the skill of your specialty. We recognize your ability and extend our wish for your continued growth in the field of art."[68] In November, Lindstrom again entered work in the Utah State Institute of Fine Arts exhibition. The *Deseret News* wrote: "By far the most gratifying response in the whole show was from the young adult amateurs' class for which Gail Lindstrom of Salt Lake won $50 with his *Young's Store*. This work has a fine rhythmic stroke used in a slightly expressionistic manner on a scene in some small village. The composition of the piece is excellent."[69] That same month Lindstrom was elected a member of the Associated Utah Artists.[70] Founded by George Martin Ottinger, a Pennsylvania-born painter and actor, the organization was dedicated to promoting a "progressive spirit in painting and sculpture by a healthy concern with new media and technique, by a spirit of mutual helpfulness, and an essentially native growth."[71] Among its members were Harwood, Stewart, and Fairbanks. Lindstrom was invited to be a guest of honor at their winter show. Dues were $4 a year, payable on January 1st. He joined.

Lindstrom participated in a show at Salt Lake's Art Barn in 1950 and invited Stewart, who praised his work. According to the *Deseret News*, as to what to do next, Lindstrom was considering following in the footsteps of his mentor: "I might go east and study, or I might find some other way to carry on my work. A lot depends on what happens between now and then."[72] Years later he would write to me: "The farther ahead one plans the more that can go wrong. So, I say, move when the spirit moves. Spirits, in my opinion, do not plan ahead." This appears to have been a long-held life philosophy.

In 1951 Stewart mentioned he had a grant to study at the Pennsylvania Academy of the Fine Arts summer school in Chester Springs, Pennsylvania. According to the school's brochure "the meandering Pickering Creek, which runs thru the property, is the life stream to hundreds of farm groups that nestle in the rolling hills with an ideal companionship between man and nature seldom equaled."[73] Lindstrom suggested to Stewart they "might go together" and offered to drive. And so they did in Lindstrom's beat-up World War II jeep. "We started out and before we arrived at the summit in Parley's Canyon [less than 20 miles from Salt Lake] the engine" overheated. Letting it cool, they added water from a nearby stream, and then endured multiple visits with mechanics at auto shops in Colorado; a mechanic in Kansas told them the brakes were too tight. The 1950s was still a time when newspapers reported on the comings and goings of local people. A Salt Lake newspaper reported, "It was all very comfy, bouncing around like tenderfeet on horseback for the first couple of days" and that Stewart "kinda got used to it" and it was "great to get our feet on the soil and meet people in their own home towns."[74] For Lindstrom, he saw parts of the country he had never seen before, a feast of places and people to draw and paint. The article concludes: "Next thing we can expect will be an organized artists posse, going across country seeking places to sketch."

In Chester Springs, along with more than 30 other students, Lindstrom and Stewart paid $40 a week for tuition, board, and room. They slept on cots and shared one bathroom in the old hospital that was once used to treat George Washington's wounded troops from Valley Forge. The pair tried to find something to paint in the surrounding countryside, "except everything was green, very green," Lindstrom wrote, disappointedly. Green, for the most part, was a color Lindstrom avoided in his work. He suggested to Stewart that they travel to Gloucester, Massachusetts, "where many American painters had worked and produced handsome paintings of the harbor and its many fishing boats." Feeling he was committed to Chester Springs, Stewart declined, and so Lindstrom drove alone to Philadelphia and along the coast to Massachusetts. Like a child artist in a paint store, upon arriving in Gloucester, Lindstrom exclaimed, "What a wonderful change!"

The sailing ships were gone but there was plenty to paint including the old buildings around the harbor and the many... colorful fishing boats. There were sections where the Italians, the Portuguese, and other nationalities had their own enclaves. All was paintable. I could let the top down on my Jeep and sit in the rear and use one of the back seats for an easel. It all worked splendidly.

His love of the ocean and salt air, in addition to the kaleidoscope of shapes and colors of boats, appealed to the young artist and would through the rest of his life, despite the fact he never learned how to swim. On his way back to Pennsylvania, Lindstrom stopped in Boston. He sold five paintings "and has promises for a one-man show in Boston next summer if he can paint and retain 40 pictures."[75] For unknown reasons, probably because he never completed that many paintings in a year, the Boston show never materialized. The following two summers, however, he returned to Gloucester to study watercolor painting with Roy Wilhelm, a professor at the Canton Art Institute and member of the American Watercolor Society.

While still a student at the University of Utah, Lindstrom had a one-man show at the Art Barn in Salt Lake City—twenty paintings of landscapes, seascapes, and sights in Virginia City, Nevada. A newspaper headline in the *Salt Lake Tribune* announcing the show called him a "Prominent Utahn..."[76] The article stated, "He uses dark colors boldly," while the *Deseret News* called Lindstrom's *Storm on East Point* a "powerful watercolor" and that Lindstrom likes working mostly with watercolor because they are "more spontaneous" and "more versatile and more adaptable." The exhibit included works from East Coast harbors, favorite haunts of Hopper. Although he tended to eschew Hopper's lyricism, Stewart painted similar subjects, including store fronts and houses adjacent to railroad tracks; in regard to the latter, the reader might note Hopper's *House by the Railroad* and *Railroad Sunset*, and Stewart's *House by the Railroad Tracks* and *House by the Tracks Near Riverdale*. Stewart said, "It is not that I love the lyrical in nature any the less, but I feel that in modern life there is not time nor inclination for it. In these pictures I'm trying to cut a slice of contemporary life as it is in the highways and byways, as I have found it...That is life, and there is nothing more interesting than life."[77] This same attitude is reflected in many works by his pupil, see for example, Lindstrom's own *House by the Track*.

Starting in 1952, Lindstrom would win nine first-place awards for his paintings at the Utah State Fair. He also won the American Watercolor Society's Winsor & Newton award (sponsored by the art supply company founded in London in 1832) for outstanding watercolor, *Late Afternoon, Oakland*, a purchase award from Watercolor U.S.A., and a number of other purchase awards at exhibitions including the Utah State Art Institute. A tally of his life-time prize money is probably less than $3000.

Chapter 11

MARRIAGE, PAINTING, & TEACHING

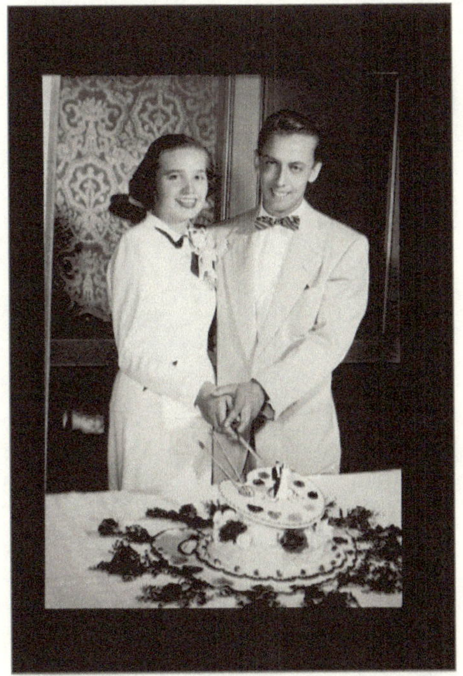

Figure 26: Wedding Day

Lindstrom graduated from the University of Utah in 1952. He had never thought of being a teacher until he reflected upon two of his favorite professors, LeConte Stewart and Alvin Gittins. "It seemed to me that they had very interesting jobs talking about art and teaching drawing and painting." In 1953 he took a job teaching art at the junior and senior high schools in Cedar City, Utah for $2650 a year. Other teachers told him he'd never make enough money to leave town. He supplemented his salary by repainting the rooms of the El Rey Motel, where he rented a room. He taught lettering, painting, drawing, basket weaving, silk screen printing, and working with tin, copper, and leather, hoping students would discover an interest in "some of them and perhaps continue." Once, early in the school day, junior high students ate the apples and bananas he brought to class as subjects for still life drawings, which caused him to scramble to find plastic fruit for later class periods. One of his former high school students told me Lindstrom was "the classiest man I ever encountered. There was an aura about him." Also that he seemed to be "in the wrong place."[78]

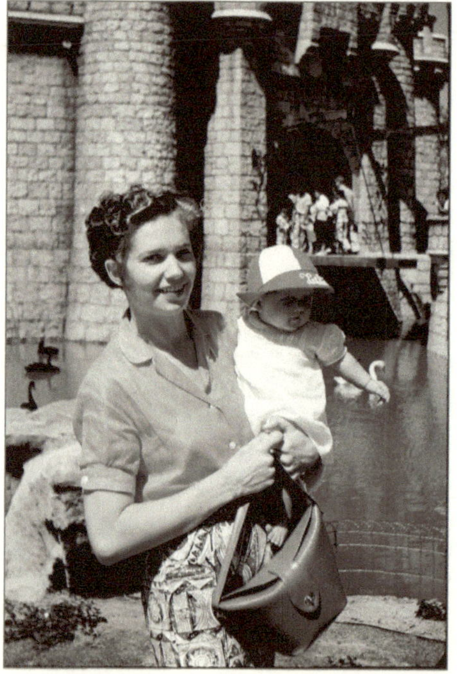

Figure 27: Marilyn Ronnow Lindstrom and daughter Leslie, 1955

Lindstrom said teaching art in Cedar City was "lonesome." As a one-man art department, he had to "do it all." In Cedar City he did befriend the dynamic Twain Tippetts, an art and theater professor at the Branch Agricultural College, later the College of Southern Utah (CSU). He accompanied Tippetts on trips to Nevada to photograph ghost towns.

On one of these trips, they stopped in Panaca to see Marilyn Ronnow, one of Tippetts' former students, who played the lead in his production of *I Remember Mama,* and later served as his assistant director, helping him take Shakespeare's plays to rural Utah schools. Shortly thereafter Lindstrom returned to Panaca for a picnic lunch with Marilyn and an exploration of the railroad and mining towns of Caliente and Pioche. She returned to college the following fall, and spent afternoons and weekends with Lindstrom and Twain and Florence Tippetts visiting scenic southern Utah spots, including the little town of New Harmony for a spectacular view of the Kolob Canyons in Zion National Park. (Lindstrom coined the term "Color Country" to describe his beloved southern Utah.) Marilyn assisted Lindstrom with a spring exhibit in Cedar City, and for her help, he gave her a painting of Butte, a Montana mining town.

After dating for a year, including a spontaneous trip to San Francisco with Bertha, they married on July 31, 1953. The wedding cake featured paint brushes and an artist's palette (figure 26). In an interview with his grandson, when asked about his most stressful experience, Lindstrom said, "Thinking about getting married was stressful and I overcame it by getting married." As a present for their first Christmas together, Lindstrom gave his new bride a watercolor of a Panaca house. In an exhibit the following year at Ray Nilson Furniture Company in Salt Lake, it was the only painting that sold. He would later paint her another one of the same house. The couple would welcome children—Leslie, Lori, Braden, and Chris—one born every three years.

The couple taught together in Salt Lake's Granite School District before returning to Cedar City, where Lindstrom secured his first college teaching job at the College of Southern Utah (now Southern Utah University), a raise—$3600 per annum—and a new apartment. They lived on the CSU campus in a barrack the school purchased and reappropriated for faculty and staff housing from Topaz, the Japanese-American internment camp in central Utah.

Stewart wrote to congratulate him:

> *I was delighted to read of your appointment as head of the art department at Cedar City... in today's news... Honors are coming to you fast these days – The recent award for your watercolor at the Capital show of the Institute of Fine Arts was well deserved – the best thing in the show – I was happy to see your talents recognized.*[79]

The college, still less than sixty years old, boasted 500 students and 40 faculty. It was now under the supervision of two men, President Daryl Chase and Director Royden Braithwaite, who became Lindstrom's friends. He designed and shot most of the photographs for the *Pageant of CSU*, the college's bulletin created for student recruitment, and, as the lone art professor, taught everything from art history and watercolor painting to jewelry making, silk screening, and ceramics. One evening, during a night ceramics class, a custodian passed through the room and noticed that Lindstrom and his students were having trouble with the clay. The custodian asked if they had wedged it. The class replied, "Wedge the clay?" He said, "Well, here I'll show you." Lindstrom recalled: "So we learned how to wedge clay and the reason for wedging clay, from one of the custodians."

Lindstrom, starved for the company of others sharing his interests, began promoting other artists. This was, perhaps, not completely unselfish. A quick study, he was always on the lookout for a good teacher. He curated the Maynard Dixon 1956 show at CSU. Dixon and his artist-wife, Edith Hamlin, owned a home in Mount Carmel, Utah, and explored and painted the American West. Dixon, who died in 1946, was surely one of the greatest of American painters, and Lindstrom referred to Dixon's *Earth Knower* (1931) as a masterpiece. Hamlin agreed to ship a collection of her late husband's paintings, drawings, and sketches to a "one stop-light" Cedar City (population ca. 6000). The Dixon exhibit contributed to the art scene in southern Utah and also allowed Lindstrom to study Dixon's actual work.

After seeing Francis de Erdely's work in California, Lindstrom invited the native Hungarian—an immigrant to the United States who had studied at prestigious art schools in Budapest, Madrid, and Paris, and would later settle in Los Angeles—to submit his work to the annual Cedar City, Utah Art Exhibit to be held on campus. De Erdely was well-known for his drawings of the downtrodden. In the *Los Angeles Times*, arts editor Arthur Millier wrote about a 1944 de Erdely exhibition in Los Angeles: "the show reaches its climax in 14 large black-and-white drawings of the horrors of war which are worthy to stand with Goya's famed *Disasters of War* etchings," while the *San Francisco Chronicle's* Alfred Frankenstein exclaimed, "They are among the most powerful drawings you will ever see."[80] De Erdely agreed to display his work in Cedar City in 1957, and thus began a friendly relationship between the two artists.

In October, 1959, Tippetts, now head of the art department at the Utah State Agricultural College (USAC) in Logan, visited de Erdely in southern California. Lindstrom encouraged Tippetts to purchase some of the Hungarian artist's work on behalf of the college. Tippetts sent his colleague Polaroids of pieces for sale and urged Lindstrom to "Rush reply air-mail!" as "this fine artist—who is coming to a dreadful end before his time and at the peak of his powers."[81] De Erdely would die a month later, November 28, 1959 at the age of 55. His work is now a part of the permanent collection at USU. I believe de Erdely's drawings and those of another contemporary artist, Charles White, inspired Lindstrom's drawings of the 1960s, all of them of people experiencing uncertain economic situations.

Lindstrom continued to display his work. Another of his university professors, George Dibble, always a champion of the arts, especially in his role as art critic for the *Salt Lake Tribune*, wrote about Lindstrom's interest in "old buildings and ghost cities," mining towns which demonstrated "touches of violent prosperity that endowed a wooden... building with a graceful facade or sensitive cornice that appeared like lace on a warrior's uniform."[82] On Lindstrom's depiction of these ghosts, in a 1954 show at the University of Utah, Dibble wrote that the artist

> *reclaims much of this hidden and grossly overlooked charm, bringing it out in startling highlights against a carefully controlled matrix of values – somber with the settling soil still betrays the violent earthy wounds of the frontier town. His ghostly highlights are startling because they are the frugally scheduled areas of white paper emerging from the deep sienna and umber that lured the miner's pick.*[83]

Lifestyle columnist Dan Valentine, also writing for the *Tribune*, called *Late Afternoon, Oakland*, "a picture that haunts you back for a second look."[84] *The New York Times* announced the Winsor & Newton win[85] and the painting was chosen to be one of fifty included in the American Watercolor Society's Annual Traveling Exhibition. Further, he was elected to Society membership. The American Watercolor Society was founded in 1866 "to promote the art of watercolor painting in America."[86] Lindstrom told a newspaper reporter, "Prior to the Renaissance, watercolor was used in Europe for sketching or for planning larger works in oil, but it wasn't considered a serious medium on its own."[87] Other members of the Society included Winslow Homer, Edward Hopper, Andrew Wyeth, Francis de Erdely, Chen Chi, and Harry Leith-Ross, who wrote from Pennsylvania to congratulate Lindstrom on his "fine picture. It has a swell design & is beautifully painted & it certainly stood out... I want you to know that I was thrilled by your picture & hope you will continue to send us many more beauties like that one."[88] The *Fort Worth Star Telegram* printed a photograph of *Late Afternoon*, announcing that "this is one of the 50 outstanding watercolors to be exhibited in a show of the 90th annual American Watercolor Society exhibition."[89]

Lindstrom began to receive even more recognition outside of Utah, selling paintings to Elmer Wellin, a collector in Chicago who later lent his name to the art museum at Hamilton College in New York, and to Senator Barry Goldwater, who purchased five pieces, including a Native American drawing as a wedding gift for his daughter, Peggy. Lindstrom displayed 13 of his works in a four-person show at the City of Paris rotunda in San Francisco. The show's curator, Beatrice Judd Ryan, belatedly wrote to inform him that four of his paintings sold, including *The Red Drape*:

> *You would have heard from me before but I tripped on an evening dress and broke my arm four weeks ago... I know you have probably had reports about the show but I wanted to emphasize that your watercolors were much liked not only by the public but by art lovers and critics.*[90]

Indeed, the celebrated *San Francisco Examiner's* art critic Alexander Fried wrote:

> *Partly because he's new here, Gaell Lindstrom, Utah water-colorist, calls up a special hurrah... His realism and his romantic love of different moods of nature speak out with extraordinary ability and freshness. Take for instance his brilliantly expressive three-dimensional "Yellow House" with its background of hill and open air; and his "Glendale Junction," with its freight train, in foreground shadow, winding through a broad desert landscape.*[91]

Also in 1957 he displayed his work in the California Watercolor Society's Annual Exhibition at the Pasadena Art Museum. Once again, apparently confused by his first name, the museum's assistant to the director wrote to "Miss Lindstrom" to inform him a painting had sold.[92] That same year Utah Governor George Clyde appointed Lindstrom a member of the Utah Institute of Fine Arts. He eventually came to the attention of H. Reuben Reynolds, an art professor at USAC in Logan, who invited him to submit work for possible purchase by the college, based on the votes of professors and art majors. The school bought *Low Tide*, which Reynolds said exhibited Lindstrom's watercolor style, "characterized by a quality of fine color and fine feeling, with an emphasis on strong shadows and highlights. The work expresses a warm feeling and fluidity of technique."[93]

In Utah Lindstrom's name would become almost synonymous with watercolor. While in graduate school he wrote an essay on the development of watercolor painting beginning with this hook: "Someone has said that there are two classes to whom watercolor painting is particularly suited—children and geniuses... Watercolor has perhaps been more abused, ignored, misused, and misunderstood than any other medium."[94] In the essay Lindstrom suggests what attracted him to watercolor: "One great advantage is brilliance and an extreme range of values from the deepest darks to the whites that only paper can give. When used fluidly it is the only medium which will do half the work for you... The fact that the pigments are so finely ground as to be transparent, lends a quality of luminosity quite unlike those in other media." Also, as he told a newspaper reporter, "I have a preference for watercolor. Perhaps because of its exasperating simplicity. It is addictive."[95]

Since 1800, after British innovations in watercolor painting, according to Lindstrom, "It remained for the Americans to make the next step in its development and ever since watercolor has largely been the American medium." Lindstrom relates the story of the movie star David Niven who, after making many films in Hollywood, returned to England, where his friend asked what he had been doing. "I've been doing pictures in America." His friend replied, "Really? Watercolors?"[96]

After Tippetts moved to Logan, he learned that the University of Utah and Brigham Young University were interested in Lindstrom's teaching services. He quickly fired off an impassioned letter to Lindstrom extolling the virtues of his new school—formerly USAC, now Utah State University—including the chance to make a real mark on a growing department, "the distinct stimulation that can come to an artist working closely with other artists,"[97] and the opportunity to teach "in the areas of your greatest strengths. We need a top water-color painter, someone who is good in ceramics and crafts, and also who enjoys working in photography." Based on the responsibilities as mentioned in this job description, the position didn't differ much from what Lindstrom was already doing in Cedar City. But Tippetts also promised to recommend a "several hundred dollars in excess of a five thousand dollar salary," no loss in academic rank, and stated that the school and department were currently "in the planning stage of our new theatre and Fine Arts Center," which appealed to Lindstrom's interest in design. In addition his friend Daryl Chase, a champion of the arts, whose name came to adorn the new fine arts center, was now in Logan as the president of the university.

After four years in Cedar City, Lindstrom accepted the position at USU. The additional money and the opportunity to work in a larger department sold him. Artists need other artists, for communion, to inspire and critique them, and to validate the pursuit of their passion, especially when they often don't receive it elsewhere.

In Logan, Lindstrom entered a sphere of diverse talent, artists from a variety of educational backgrounds who won local and national awards: abstract painter Everett Thorpe, watercolorist Harrison Groutage (Grout), photographer R.T. Clark, naturalistic printmaker Moishe Smith, and modernist sculptor Larry Elsner. About the older Thorpe, who reconstructed bugs on a canvas and had studied with Hans Hofmann, Lindstrom said, "Ev had all the talent in the world. He could do anything—portraits, landscapes, figure studies, sports cartoons. A great abstractionist." Thorpe became a mentor, while the Falstaffian Grout, who also taught painting, was a training partner and friend "right at the start." Arriving later was printmaker and painter Adrian Van Suchtelen, the highly-versatile, Indonesian-born artist, who is still creating.

Further, a brilliant pianist played a few doors away. Irving Wasserman was the first professor of piano at USU, and for Lindstrom both an inspiration and patron. As war was brewing in Europe, Wasserman escaped from his native Poland in 1938, arriving in Logan on the bus with a dollar in his pocket. He championed other pianists through the Wasserman Music Festival and commissioned Lindstrom to do a painting of the Logan train depot for his young son, Paul, who loved trains.

USU's most famous alum and Lindstrom's friend, Ardeshir Zahedi, a former Iranian Ambassador to the United States, would call the university the place "where I was reborn." It would prove to be "the right place" for Lindstrom, allowing him to grow and stretch as an artist.

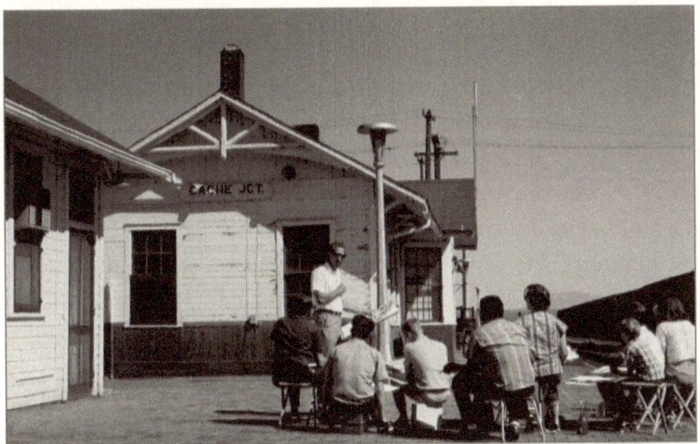

Figure 28: Lindstrom teaching on site, Cache Junction, Utah, 1960s

Tippetts, who my siblings and I came to call "Uncle Twain," sold Lindstrom a piece of property for a house in North Logan, near enough to USU that Lindstrom could ride his bicycle to campus. Lindstrom taught ceramics, art history, and painting, training many future art teachers and artists, including Osral Allred, Stephen Naegle, Del Parson, Andy Watson, Kathleen Torgesen Murdock, Mary McDonald, Susan Harris, and Gary Case, many of whom would later inspire generations of young Utah artists. He impressed upon his students the elements (line, shape, texture, value, light, color) and principles (emphasis and dominance, balance, repetition, contrast, opposition, harmony, transition) of design: "Elements are the material things you have to work with" and principles are "how you deal with the elements… to shape your ideas." Murdock recalled, "He taught us how to have a center of interest that led the eye around the painting and back to the center of interest. He would take a specific color like Paynes Grey and show us exactly how we could use it to make other colors sing by what we put next to it." Lindstrom "loved the white of the paper and showed us how to preserve it in the right places to make the painting sparkle."[98] Following the lead of the French impressionists, he took his students out of the classroom to paint on site in San Miguel de Allende, Mexico and Park City and Cache

Valley, Utah. Murdock wrote, "I still love to ride through the Logan area because we painted every old barn through the whole valley. He also loved to take us to the old pioneer houses with their big porches and numerous chimneys. He showed us how to keep painting even though the light kept changing, and the colors and the patterns changing with the light."[99]

One former student wrote of him: "The best watercolor teacher I had in many classes at USU & U of U. The best."[100] Another student wrote: "Because of him I learned to love looking [for] and seeing art and beauty."[101] Harris, a potter, recalled: "He doesn't try to influence a student's work. He doesn't tell you exactly what to do. He says, 'try it. See what happens.' He gives suggestions and encouragement, and says, 'do what you want to do and we'll talk about it.'"[102] Andy Watson said that Lindstrom led by watching where his students were going. "You take what they are seeing and you help them see it."[103]

Watson first met Lindstrom in 1971 at an "amazing," month-long USU ceramic workshop in Vernal, Utah. Angelo Garzio, an extraordinary potter, and professor at Kansas State University, demonstrated pottery-making while Lindstrom lectured on design. Watson said that Lindstrom "wasn't a producing potter. He was producing potters." A few years later, with a plan to earn an MFA in ceramics, Watson arrived in Logan with just enough money for a one-night stay at a motel. Lindstrom gave him a paid teaching assistantship. Lindstrom "treated me," he said, "as if I was already something."

Together they created a rubric to evaluate student work, based on three criteria: craftsmanship, design and function, and creative expression and inventiveness. The students also evaluated their own work using the same rubric. This was typical Lindstrom. He wanted his students to be engaged at every level. When he showed his TA a Shoji Hamada piece glazed smooth on the inside with a rough glaze on the outside, Watson asked how Hamada did it. Lindstrom simply replied: "Andy, see if you can duplicate it." And he did.

During a master's class, one student, concerned like his peers with a forthcoming thesis show that would determine whether or not they would graduate, asked Lindstrom a question about preparing for it. Lindstrom dove into a description of the basic elements and principles of design. "That's not what I want," the student said, but his professor calmly proceeded with his description. The student stormed out of the room. This was a teaching moment Watson never forgot, and reminded him of his own father's experience with an impatient farmer. For these two wise men, the question was: "What do I know that this man doesn't?" Watson said, "the key to Gaell Lindstrom is this: you've got to get back to the basics. If you want to find something new, you can only find it when you're on solid ground."

When Watson previewed for Lindstrom and Van Suchtelen thirty pots for his own masters show, they said, "these are just pots" and they won't work for a show. Lindstrom liked the forms but they didn't have "tongues to talk" and "they don't capture space." Watson replied, "Why didn't you tell me that before," but he knew they were "afraid of guiding me too much." He took a hammer to the pots. "They wanted me," he said, "to express something of myself, my feelings, emotions, and ideas." He went back to work. Because he had only two weeks before the announced show, everything he created was salt-glazed, which required only a single firing. One piece that made the final show was titled *Hot Air*. People holding it could rest their noses on the lip of the pot, blow air through a tiny hole, pause, and then hear a rush of wind. It was a comment on the hot air we all sometimes exhale. Watson, who would go on to become an award-winning ceramics teacher, told me, "as you get better" as an artist "your students will follow." He recalled a visit to Lindstrom's campus office, discovering the artist at his easel and all the lights turned off. Only a little sunlight filtered in through a window. He asked, "Why are you painting in the dark?" Lindstrom replied, "You

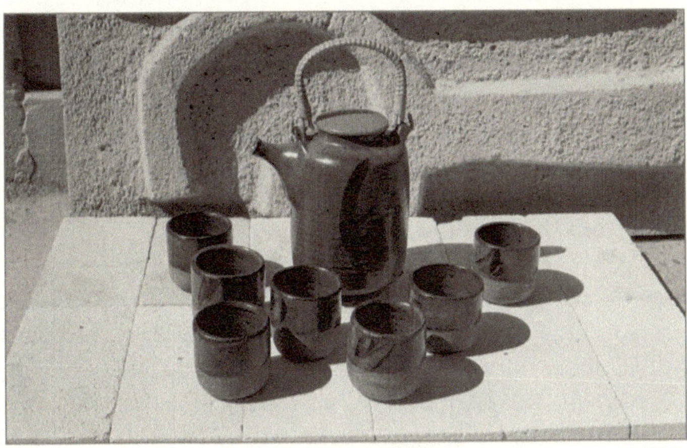

Figure 29: Pottery by Lindstrom, ca. 1962

have to make it more brilliant because the room's dark. What I make will show brighter in the light." This may explain why "he always wore his sunglasses but he would paint the colors out in the open with glow and accuracy."[104]

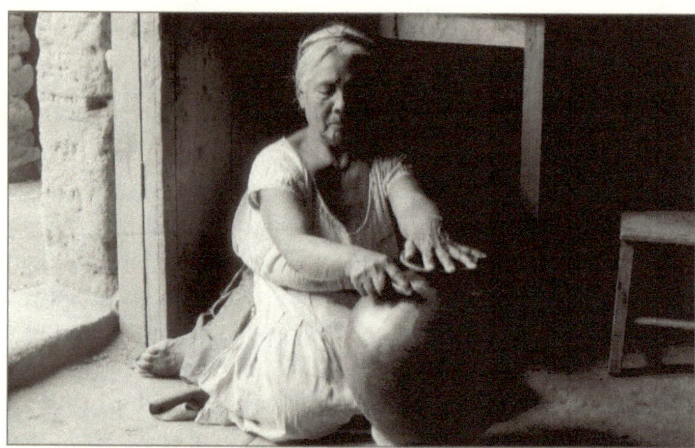

Figure 30: potter Sophrina Mateo at work, photograph by Lindstrom

"Your father changed my life," Watson told me. "I was his piece of clay. He made me a good teacher. And he made skilled enough that I could spend the rest of my life making pottery."

Despite more recognition outside of Utah, Lindstrom would never leave his sparsely populated, mostly rural native state. He did, however, take whatever opportunity afforded itself to promote the arts in Utah and get his own work in front of the public. Lindstrom's watercolor *Park City* took first place in the Thirty-fifth Annual Spring Salon at the Springville Art Museum. A Lindstrom desert photograph and a painting of Brigham Young's Salt Lake City home would don the covers of the *Improvement Era*, an LDS monthly magazine.

In 1962, from the California College of Arts and Crafts in Oakland, Lindstrom earned his only graduate degree—an MFA in ceramics. He choose ceramics over painting "because I thought at the time that a degree in painting was somewhat like a degree in playing the piano. In other words, not really necessary to have a degree to succeed." For his thesis, *Development of Clay Bodies and Glazes from Natural Deposits Occurring in Utah, Southern Idaho, and Northern Arizona* (1963), Lindstrom roamed the American West, digging for clays he would use to create pottery that accompanied his written text (figure 29). He later produced and directed a film for public television titled *Mateo: Potter of San Bartolo de Coyotepec*, featuring Ernesto Mateo and his wife Sophrina, of black pottery fame (figure 30).

In his first year in Logan, Lindstrom worked on revising "the art curriculum which was poorly organized and… incomplete. Later I complained so much about the graduate program that I was assigned to rewrite it"; he would direct the program for most of his career at the university.

At the time the art facilities at the school were third rate at best. Class-rooms were housed in the basement of the administration building, Old Main, while ceramics courses met in an abandoned heating plant. Once, a guest instructor, after igniting a kiln, lost control of the fire, which quickly ate up the wooden roof. Classes continued to meet in the same location until late in the autumn when it grew too cold. USU was a land-grant school, with majors in animal husbandry. Lindstrom noticed a barn for livestock that sat on a prime campus spot. Why not make it an art barn? The sheep vacated the premises, a new concrete floor was poured, a third floor added along with a fire-proof kiln, and presto: drawing classes were taught on the top floor, sculpture on the second, and ceramics on the ground floor. It became the university's best art facility at the time. Meanwhile, the prestige of the art programs and department faculty was growing. The state would later provide

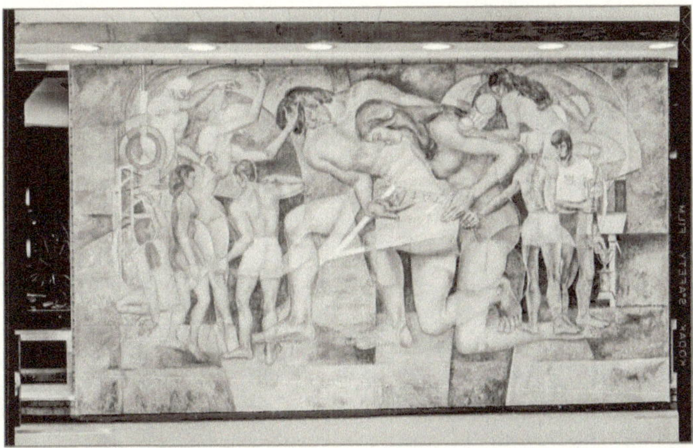

Figure 31: USU physical education mural by Ev Thorpe, Harrison

funds for a new art facility, theater, and concert hall, all linked by common entryways and wide hallways.

There was still much to learn. Lindstrom conducted experiments on Utah clays, from 70 clay beds, to learn about their potential use in pottery. He was delighted to discover "all colors imaginable in Utah clays...." In the early 1960s, he collaborated with Ev Thorpe to create large murals for the university's library, forestry/biological science, and physical education buildings (in this last instance assisted by Grout) (figure 31). Thorpe was an abstract painter and Grout was primarily a realist painter. All three men appreciated both forms, and their murals reflect this.

The Picasso-esque mural in the library (figure 31) with its flat planes and sharp angles, depicted the history of the book. The university stated in a press release:

> *Several things can be identified, although there has been no attempt by the artists to portray any object in its regular form... Rosetta Stone, Cuneiform figures, the quill and scroll of the medieval monks... the crude tools of the Babylonian and Egyptian civilization... an early printing press together with the block letters used in it... the Dead Sea Scrolls and an owl, the Egyptian symbol of the letter M.*[105]

Significantly, the mural was painted on the east wall and in content emphasizes the Eastern Hemisphere's significant contribution to

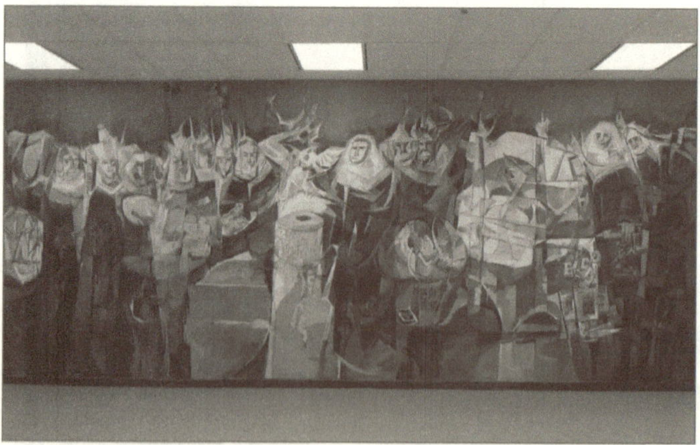

Figure 32: USU library mural

written communication through its images. In creating it, Lindstrom and Thorpe used a slide projector thirty feet away to impose their drawing on the blank wall, traced the drawing, and then painted it. The English department was located in the library, so as a student I saw the striking mural almost every day: the many spear-like lines and the silent, hooded figures, seemingly unaware of each other—cloistered lives captured and displayed together—look at the viewer, or down in

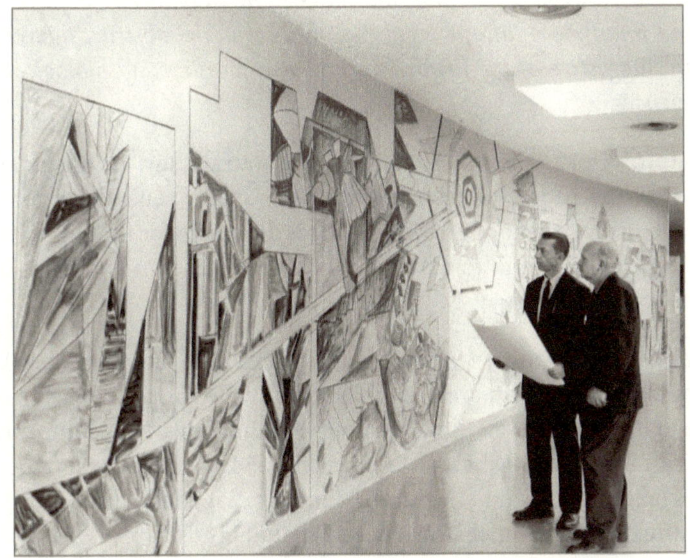

Figure 33: Lindstrom and Thorpe planning USU science mural

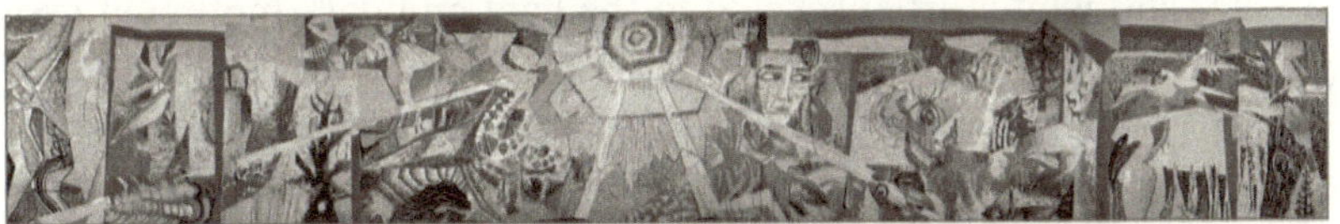

Figure 34: USU forestry/biological science mural

judgment at the tools of the book, as if its invention was a somber affair. The United States State Department recognized it "as a distinguished work of art, and pictures of it were distributed throughout Europe."[106]

The science mural may be the jewel in the crown (figures 33 and 34). Leith-Ross would call *The Divine Light of Intelligence Illuminating Man's Studies of Nature* a "grand accomplishment."[107] At the time it was the largest mosaic mural in the Intermountain West: 10 feet tall and 54 feet long. Thorpe and Lindstrom created a small scale drawing, enlarged and traced it in charcoal on the curved wall, applied a heavy adhesive, and then, along with art students, set on the wall, one by one, more than a quarter million, Italian artisan-chipped tiles. Clearly visible in the front of the building, the Logan newspaper, *Herald Journal*, described it as follows:

> *The subject is a central sun... with its rays reaching out to primitive vegetation and animals, more advanced lifeforms, and finally to man and creatures of his era. The abstract figures are suggestive of the lifeforms studied in forestry and biological sciences...*[108]

The university's brochure claimed the mural's sun "is intended to symbolize the source of cosmic fire... periodically renewed, a refining and redemptive agent of great power. It is an image for that light which both inspires the mind to adventure into the unknown and helps burn the shadows and mist away."[109]

In 1973 Craig Law, a student of Lindstrom's who later became a USU photography professor, created a black and white image of the artist at home in his North Logan studio (figure 35). In the vertical composition, Law's camera is slightly below the artist, now 54 years old. In soft focus, a canvas takes up a third of the image, running diagonally through almost the entire composition. A brush in each hand, Lindstrom sits at his easel looking into the camera lens. One side of the artist's face is in the light, the other in shadow, although the division is uneven. Lindstrom's black sweater and white turtleneck add to the light and dark motif. On first glance the picture may appear static, but it's filled with diagonal lines: canvas, pant leg, paint brush, veins of a hand, and the scar-like wrinkles below the artist's eyes. The face makes us linger—mouth closed, lips turned into a faint smile, inviting eyes. Lose the paint brushes and the easel and you might say he looks like a kindly uncle on a Postum break. He had that 1950s Jimmy Stewart-in-the-movies look. The photograph captures a look as familiar to his family as his art.

In August 1973, Lindstrom was a guest artist at the University of Minnesota-Duluth where he conducted an advanced painting workshop. Cheng-Khee Chee, a student in the workshop, became a close friend. Chee later exhibited his own work around the world and illustrated the award-winning children's book *Old Turtle*. In announcing a show of the

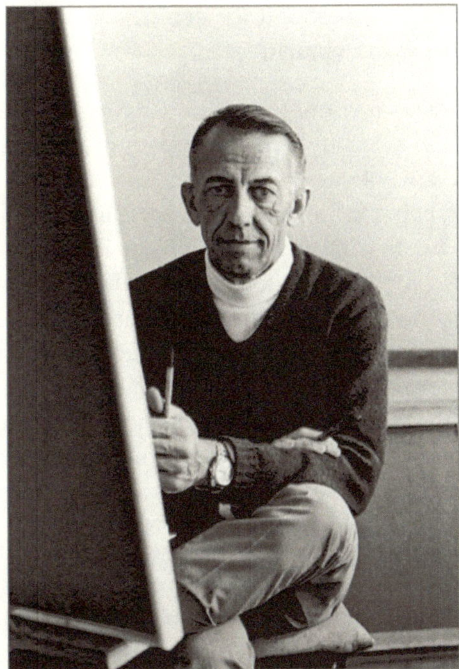

Figure 35: Lindstrom in his North Logan studio, 1973

student paintings that came out of the workshop, the *Duluth Herald* identified Lindstrom as "a nationally known painter."[110] If this was true at the time, it was probably only within a tight circle of artists and art enthusiasts.

That same year he spent part of a sabbatical studying in Mashiko, Japan with Tatsuzō Shimaoka, a potter and former student of Shoji Hamada. Shimaoka was declared a "Living National Treasure" in 1996. The Japanese potter's work can appear rough hewn or exquisitely polished, but always beautiful. He pioneered a process called "Jōmon zogan," in which the artist uses a rope or cord to make decorative impressions in the clay and then a slip is inlaid into the impression, highlighting the decoration and giving the piece texture.[111] Other than a few photographs, there is nothing that survives to describe Lindstrom's experience in Japan. He was still teaching ceramics in Logan and he needed a teacher; Shimaoka was one of the world's best potters, so Lindstrom went to Mashiko. Lindstrom never imitated Shimaoka, but I believe his life-long quest for beauty was satiated for a few months. Further, Shimaoka was a restless artist who designed kilns, experimented with clays from around the country, and varied his processes; in short, an artist worth emulating.

In 1975 Lindstrom wrote to Leslie, "I have been teaching the same thing for about 14 years and am a bit weary of so much repetition and could even use a whole new career—or just paint and leave it at that." Upon returning home from Japan, he tried selling his own pottery. Lindstrom opened his first business, Bear Lake Pottery, with a storefront in Garden City on the shores of northern Utah's most beautiful lake. In addition to pottery, he sold his photographs of the lake and Guatemalan tapestries. As children, although the gorgeous but twisty, 40-mile drive through Logan Canyon to get to Bear Lake sometimes caused car sickness, my siblings and I spent countless hours exploring the lake in all four seasons. Lindstrom loved Logan Canyon and, since he never learned to swim, I suspect the drive to the lake was as much the point.

Long interested in Native Americans and, after numerous trips to southern Utah and his own historical research, Lindstrom produced a portfolio of charcoal pencil drawings of Washakie, chief of the Shoshones; Ouray, chief of the Uncompahgre Utes; three Navajos; and

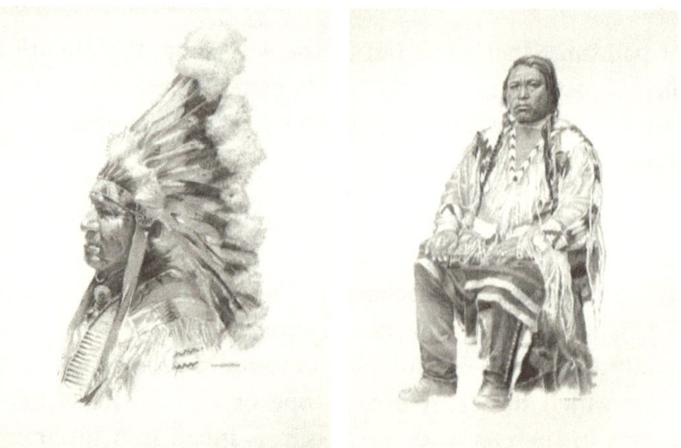

Figure 36: Chief Washakie and Chief Ouray

a Plains Native American (figure 36). He told a newspaper reporter, "I feel that both Washakie and Ouray were men who have not received the recognition due them" and that he completed the portfolio "to add to the enjoyment of these great peoples and add to the understanding of their past and hopes for the future."[112]

Ever the teacher, Lindstrom's Bear Lake Pottery business card, after identifying multiple uses of the pottery including "the baking of casseroles" and "breads" read: "Often pottery is enjoyed, however, for its beauty and the pleasure it gives... The origin of the art of pottery is lost in prehistory but it remains today, as thousands of years ago, man's most useful art and craft." Lindstrom made enough money to pay expenses but little more. He did befriend Brian Swinton, principal partner in Sweetwater, Inc., a large, real-estate development on the lake's south end, who agreed to exchange a parcel of land meant for a cabin on a mountain overlooking the lake for a number of Lindstrom paintings. Forty years later I would find myself photographing four of these paintings on Swinton's front porch in Virginia for the book *The Art of Gaell Lindstrom.*

To his children, Lindstrom often extolled the virtues of higher education. Leslie would be the first to graduate. She earned a degree in dance from the University of Utah. Lindstrom wrote to her:

> *I have decided it best to develop as many [talents] as well as one can even if he isn't the world's best something or other. It is always quite a shock to find otherwise brilliant people who know almost nothing of the breadth of what there is to learn because of their lack of peripheral vision. Always looking into a narrow tunnel is hardly worthy of being an education.*

All four of his children earned graduate degrees.

In several photographs of Lori as a child, she has her arm around one of her siblings, as if protecting them. Lindstrom advised her to focus on the young, not the old who have already lived their lives. She works as a high school advisor and runs summer camps in the Colorado Rockies for children of military families.

Lindstrom's first major solo exhibit occurred in March, 1973 at USU. In a press release the school described the artist as "a highly self-critical perfectionist."[113] In a letter to Lindstrom, Tippetts called the show "one of the important art events in the history of our school."[114] He wrote of the artist's "reluctance to be honored with a one-man exhibit," acknowledging "you are not one to selfishly seek publicity and recognition." The show, featuring 30 watercolors as well as photographs of Kane Creek (a tributary of the Colorado River near Moab, Utah) was a big hit according to some of the 300 people in attendance at the opening. Tippetts informed the artist that 15 paintings sold within the first few days of the show, which "should reassure you of your pre-show doubts." Paintings on display included *Orange Buoy, View of Toledo,* and *Beached.* George Dibble claimed that some of the work resulted from Lindstrom's study with Chen Chi.[115]

Most important to Lindstrom's art at this time was his friendship with Chi, the master watercolorist. Born in Wuxi, China in 1912, Chi immigrated to the United States in 1947, spending most of his adult life in New York City where he painted street, park, and theater scenes in epic style. He displayed his work throughout the United States, China, and in a one-man retrospective show at Versailles. No stranger to Utah, having worked as an artist-in-residence for Ogden City Schools in 1967 through a U.S. federal grant introducing students to great American artists, Chi returned four years later to be artist-in-residence at USU. Grout said, "Having Chen Chi on campus is like having a Heifetz or a Shakespeare in the academic community."[116] Pearl Buck once said of Chi, "… in spite of the inherent delicacy of his medium, he is able to present with amazing power the elemental forces of nature, wherein man assumes his proportionate place."[117] I remember Chi visiting our home and silently watching the way he would accept with both hands a small bowl my father handed him to inspect, and how he listened more than he talked. Lindstrom wrote that Chi sold almost everything he paints, "but is still very unaffected by any success he has enjoyed."

In describing the necessary preparation for the early "gentle-man-painters in China," artist and historian Diana Kan could have been talking about Chi and Lindstrom: "They had the cultural background for mature, philosophical thought, and their artistic sensibilities had been heightened by long nurturing of an appreciation for beauty and harmony."[118] Until the student acquired the knowledge and skill necessary, Kan wrote, it was important to copy a master to learn and to perpetuate "ancient rules and techniques which might otherwise be lost."[119] Tippetts said Lindstrom's friendship and study with Chi "resulted not in imitation but in a new and challenging synthesis...."[120] Chi's influence on Lindstrom's work is unmistakable; see, for example, the colorful, impressionist *Along the Li River,* the setting dwarfing the tiny human figures. Some of Lindstrom's forest scenes, with their prominent tree branches or explosions of leafy color, also show Chi's influence. Lindstrom said, "I hope I don't imitate the Chinese painters in my work. But when you use the same papers and materials, you're bound to have some similarities, whether you want them or not."[121] Lindstrom soon became an enthusiastic fan of Chinese watercolor paper. He told a *Herald Journal* reporter: "The fibers of the paper from rice straw take watercolor beautifully, producing a soft edge which is ideally adapted for the painting of nature. With these materials, effects can be achieved which you can't get any other way."[122]

China also produced many other great watercolor painters. So, of course, Lindstrom had to go. The highlight of his first trip was Guilin. For someone who grew up in the shadow of the Wasatch Range, it's easy to understand Lindstrom's attraction to Guilin and its surreal karst mountains, many rising sharply and singularly from the valley floor, with trees growing vertically and horizontally. Along with rice paddies, villages woven around their feet, and the gentle Li River lined with bamboo groves, these mountains create perhaps the most iconic image of China. Lindstrom would never attempt to capture them realistically on canvas—"hard to improve on what you can see."

Historically the Chinese painted from inspiration and since the ninth century the subject of art shifted from human to nature.[123] A story goes that the emperor asked the master painter Wu Tao-tze to paint a favorite mountain and river. The painter visited the site. "When he returned and was asked for his sketches, he replied, 'I have it all in my heart,' and then, in a single day, he threw off a hundred miles of landscape."[124] Lindstrom's Chinese paintings are experiments in form and color and lean toward non-representational, although most suggest some kind of mountainscape. In looking at this work, one could say he followed Wu Tao-tze or the eleventh-century Chinese painter Su Shih: "To paint the bamboo one must have it entirely within one. Grasp the brush, look intently [at the paper], then visualize what you are going to paint. Follow your vision quickly, lift your brush and pursue directly that which you see, as a falcon dives on the springing hare—the least slackening and it will escape you."[125]

In Guilin, Lindstrom met two child artists, Li Yen and her brother Li Yang. The family lived in a small apartment, "but made space for the children to paint in the daytime, putting what appeared to be a 4' x 8' sheet of plywood over a bed," Lindstrom wrote. Li Yang "would paint a picture of a horse, a favorite Chinese subject anciently as well as today, by starting with the rear hoof. A most unusual approach, but he still managed to… end up with a horse in good proportions." Lindstrom called one of Yen's landscapes "a wonderful work and very large." He suggested the children "ought to be sent to an art school where they might blossom into great artists." Their parents replied, "if 'it' is in them they will blossom."

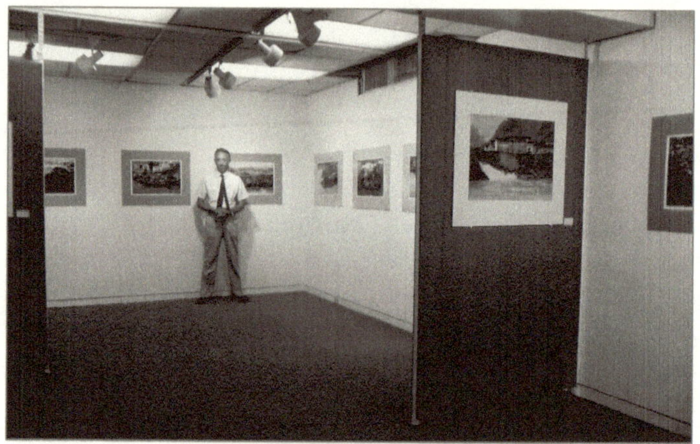

Figure 37: American Library Show, Hong Kong

Lindstrom took private lessons from a Hong Kong painter, who was a "traditionalist" in his approach to landscapes. Later, while in Taipei, he spotted from the street a second-floor art gallery displaying the paintings of Koo Mei. Originally from mainland China—her family fled the country in 1949—the artist, before she became a painter, was a professional singer and movie star in Hong Kong and Bangkok. Her brother, Joseph Koo, composed the scores of many films including Bruce Lee's *The Way of the Dragon*. Lindstrom eagerly climbed the stairs in Taipei. "Her work was just what I hoped to find though it was entirely new to me… more modern than traditional works but still retained a Chinese flavor." He purchased one, later learning that his artist-friend Liu Kuo-sung knew Koo Mei. Liu arranged a visit to her high-rise apartment in Hong Kong. Lindstrom asked if she would "show me the manner in which her watercolors were done. She graciously consented and I did learn much that afternoon. She later in the week finished the started painting and gave it to me." His paintings such as *Mountain Kolobs*, created from his imagination although named after the famous sandstone formations in Zion National Park, demonstrate her influence. At Lindstrom's invitation Koo Mei conducted a watercolor workshop at USU and he gave her a tour of Utah and Wyoming's mountain wonders.

In China and in Hong Kong's Aberdeen area, Lindstrom captured on film many subjects that he would put to canvas and offer to the public in a show at the American Library in Hong Kong in 1982. Later he would host the show "Fifty Photographs" of Guilin, China in the basement of our house.

After retiring from Utah State in June of 1984, he returned to China that same month. In his typical modest style, he wrote in a journal: "I hope to find a painter of the Po Mo (free approach or big splash!) [style] and hope to finally learn and paint something of some importance in some aspect." Along the way he stopped in San Francisco to see the exhibits of Grant Wood and Robert Motherwell. About Wood he wrote, "He died at 50 and at 65 I've not started yet! Not much time left." In Hangzhou, he studied at the Zhejiang Art Academy, staying in the dorms, and meeting up with Cheng-Khee Chee and his students from the University of Minnesota-Duluth. Despite the gracious hospitality of people at the Academy, Lindstrom believed the trip was mostly a failure. It rained almost unceasingly, papers he bought absorbed the ink too fast, he accidently splashed ink in his eye, which

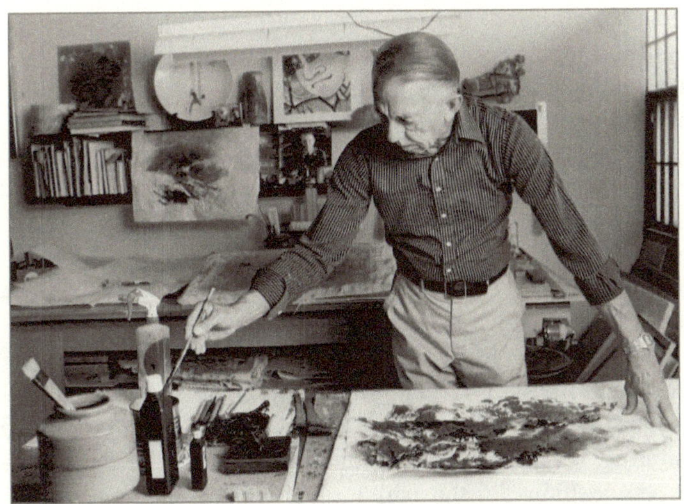

Figure 38: Lindstrom in his studio, 1984

obscured his sight for a time, and finally, he was unsuccessful in finding a good teacher. "I learned little about painting or printmaking as all faculty members seem to be doing very academic work which was not very exciting and like I did about 40 years ago. This is not to say that there was no competence but there just was really no spark... Innovation is not encouraged and even frowned upon from official circles." He found one professor, since retired, a friend of Chi's, in his small apartment "painting a sort of propaganda-type work in oil of some soldiers."

He did, however, make it to Wuxi, Chi's birthplace. A travel agent picked him up and took him to her office in town "through 1000s of bicycles—the car was no match for them." The next day he visited the 500 year-old Ling Bridge: "I had my driver come to the top to take a Polaroid of me which naturally was a crowd stopper—about 50 people crowded but close to see the print develop and all with awesome expressions of awe." An old man carrying a baby asked in English if he was taking "colored pictures... When he saw my print develop he asked for a picture of him and likely as not his gr. gr. grandchild, so I made quite a nice one for him and the crowd was further entertained and laughing." Later he toured the Grand Canal in "the Dragon boat," 100 feet long, a crew of five, and one passenger—no other tours that day. "People step out of their backdoors and wash clothes in the canal and kids swim in it..."

China also inspired his mixed media pieces such as *Night Forms*, probably his most abstract work. Upon returning from Asia, he installed a skylight in his studio, extending the time he could paint on winter and cloudy days. In an article for the *Salt Lake Tribune*, which displayed a photograph of him painting a Chinese-style watercolor (figure 38), he said, "I feel I'm still trying to learn something. I haven't learned anything yet. I have yet to do any significant painting, but I'm eager to learn."[126]

He wrote to Leslie: "Here I am almost 66 and still looking for a good painting teacher!" However inadequate he may have felt, in 1986, the Nora Eccles Harrison Museum of Art at Utah State University honored the artist with the show "Gaell Lindstrom," his first retrospective exhibition. One of my favorite works from this show is *Duluth Ramp*. About this painting, Lindstrom said he put all of the city's dock area together in one composition. For the exhibition program, George Dibble wrote: "When I hear the name Gaell Lindstrom, I think of watercolor... Gaell knows no language better than aquarelle."[127] Of the 76 paintings—the earliest from 1947, *Young's Store*—70 were watercolors. Video from opening night shows a large crowd, many waiting for the attention of the artist, who one would never spot by his clothes: a beige suitcoat and trousers. For most of the evening, he stood with his back to the paintings, letting them speak for themselves, but also, I think, with that constant, nagging feeling that he could do better. Whenever I glanced at Lindstrom, he was in the same place, surrounded by people. I don't believe he sat down the entire night. My mother sent him flowers, along with this note: "Thanks for all the beauty you've brought into my life."

When the show concluded in June, although he didn't always stay at home, he tried to make up for lost time. He wrote to his childhood friend, Bill Richards: "FAMILY is number one. It pales all else I have frittered away my life on."

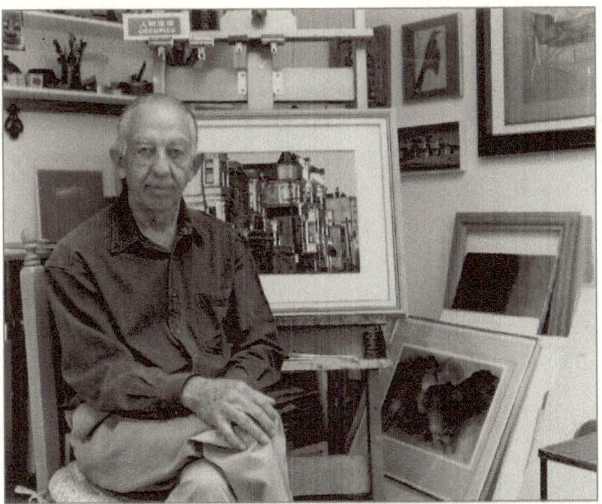
Figure 39: Lindstrom in his "Blue Door Studio" 1996

In retirement Lindstrom continued to do what came naturally: He traveled, often with family. In 1996, my parents flew to Madrid and rented a car. "We had no set itinerary but just drove as we pleased mostly on country roads and photographing everything looking interesting enough for a painting. Marilyn drove while I often left the car and roamed in small towns or narrow gravel roads." On a road twisting its way up to the old section of Toledo, he cried, "stop here." Mom did and he hopped out with his camera. The traffic backed up, so he said, "Just come back around." She could have killed him. Instead she drove off, terrified she'd never find the way back. She did.

Because a friend told Lindstrom about a trip to Morocco, he "had been interested ever since," and so, along with my brother and I, he flew to Casablanca. The trip highlights included Fez's biblical-era medina and the seacoast city of Essaouira where Orson Welles had filmed his *Othello*.

With heavy hearts, my parents sold the home where they raised their children and moved to southern Utah's Apple Valley, about 30 miles northeast of Saint George. They built an adobe-style, stucco home and studio with the assistance of a young crew from the nearby polygamist community of Colorado City, Arizona. Lindstrom continued to paint, although he abandoned experimentation. Needing extra income, he made his best marketing decision: like his mentor, LeConte Stewart, he would paint in oil, but unlike Stewart, he took as subjects dramatic landscapes, all in southern Utah including the West Temple in Zion. Lindstrom envisioned, like van Gogh, a "studio of the south."[128] Grout would build a similar but larger home on the adjacent lot. Across the street lived the Fuentes: Marlene, who worked in television and film, and Paul, a fine artist, who once drew movie posters and created lobby displays for Los Angeles film palaces. Friends, artists, and strangers would visit. He rescued a French family, the Logeais, who had run out of gas after sightseeing in the Park. Unsurprisingly, they became fast friends and would later host Lindstrom and I in Paris.

Utah Governor Norman Bangerter appointed Lindstrom to the Utah Arts Council. One of its primary responsibilities was awarding grants to artists and art organizations. The Union Pacific Railroad had recently deeded its depot to Utah to become the first art museum owned by the state. In this role on the Council, Lindstrom championed the project, but it never happened. Today the depot hosts weddings and other events.

In 1998, in a one-man show at the Saint George Art Museum, he exhibited and sold several paintings.

After ten years, the Lindstroms moved to Saint George to be closer to doctors and grocery stores. They bought an ordinary rambler, then surrounded it with oleanders that sported white and pink flowers, red yucca, purple Russian sage, yellow perky sue, and a single, flowering plum tree. Lindstrom continued to paint, hung up his international traveling jacket, and enjoyed sitting in the backyard soaking up the desert sun. When one of the yuccas grew a five-foot flower, a delighted Lindstrom said, "I can't believe it."

Chapter 12

LATER LIFE & FAREWELL

Upon reflection, I was only detained in Urumqi, China, and I did ignore the voice in my head that admonished, "Keep walking." However, I cannot overstate Lindstrom's influence on my life. My mother tells me I'm so much like him it's uncanny. Mannerisms, speech, many personal interests, my teaching, views on politics, and tastes in art are all strongly shaped by my father. One evening after his retirement, he gave me a special screening and art lecture. I learned the necessity of some form of opposition—a tree, the edge of a building—to keep the viewer within the composition; too much harmony equals sameness, too much variety is chaos; cool colors recede, warm colors advance; best to seek an informal balance; and the sun takes on the color of whatever it strikes. He told me to avoid matinee movies—I'd waste the sunlight— and he reminded me each spring that the days were starting to get longer.

I miss our photography sessions at the kitchen table. In addition to cropping, he would always twist and turn my photos to "find an abstraction," to see "how many pictures one can find in a single photograph," squinting his eyes at a rooftop in Istanbul or a market in Bac Ha, Vietnam. "All good compositions are abstract." Abstraction freed one from the tyranny of a picture always having to look like something in nature, and silenced those who look at a painting and say, "it doesn't look like that in real life." When I emailed him a batch of photographs of a floating village in Cambodia, he wrote back: "Try looking at the one of small boats and a lone man on one in the extreme left. View it upside down!" It always took me a minute to see what he could see in an instant. He had the ability to completely eliminate distractions of thought and vision, and focus lazer-like on an image. Most of what I learned about photographic composition, I learned at home. But what I remember feeling is Lindstrom's contagious excitement about seeing photographs of places he had never been.

I decided to major in English not only because I loved my general education courses, but also to separate myself to some degree from Lindstrom, although I find myself talking about the "art of a novel" or encouraging students to take film seriously as an art form. When I started working with pre-service teachers, Lindstrom gave me Katherine Kuh's article "The Fine Arts" from *The Saturday Review*, about the training of art teachers. She wrote that "the fine arts cannot properly be separated from the other arts. Painting, poetry, music, the dance, all stem from common roots."[129] Lindstrom gave me an idea that later became a project for my composition students at Utah Valley State College (UVSC): Write a short monologue as a famous artist and then perform it for the class. The project wasn't exactly new, as William Luce's *The Belle of Amherst* proves, but the students, rather than confined to a choice of writers, could pick an artist who worked in any medium. The students wrote and performed monologues as van Gogh, Ludwig van Beethoven, and Martha Graham. Most of the students had never acted before, but many of the performances were brilliant. That summer I asked "Eugene O'Neill" and "James Thurber" to perform in my Orem, Utah living room for my parents in honor of Lindstrom's birthday.

Lindstrom told me that "learning about anything can be exciting." He wrote:

> *Rewards for your time as a teacher are not well measured in salary. We all know they are way too small for what is required of you. So, one must look at the greatest challenge, making the lives richer of those students put into your care. Rewards from touching lives are not measurable but the opportunity to do so is greatest in the classroom. But, they are real and they are there and last lifetimes.*

A master typist and proponent of any technology that allowed him to do something more quickly, Lindstrom came to love email. The medium proved to be perfect for his pithy sense of humor. When I taught at Brigham Young University-Hawai'i, he wrote to me:

> *Just thought up a student exercise. Have them write a story, news item, whatever, in Shakespeare English! If they don't know any, assign some Bible reading or even some Shakespearean reading? Or, if you have an advanced group, say English 102, have them write it in Chaucer's English. These two ideas should*

keep your class size within very reasonable limits but may also keep you unemployed.

When I complained about teaching two introductory writing courses that same semester, he suggested:

I have finally learned that it is a "performance" on the part of the professor that students remember and if you can interject just a little something they might benefit from, you are a remarkable teacher. I suggest you start over and teach some aspect of, say, art studio. If a student hacked off a finger or swallowed some paint thinner you could just send them to the dispensary, dismiss class, and spend the rest of the day enjoying yourself.

When my sister was preparing to teach fourth grade, he wrote: "Don't worry about school starting soon as I have a simply great rock collection for you with which you can get through at least 6 months of this school year without really being prepared in anything else."

One of his friends and collectors, Mike Larsen, moved from Logan to the far north. In October of 2002, Lindstrom emailed:

Dear Braden, many thanks for the email and contents. One [item] goes to Mike in Alaska who has been in school for about two weeks and is enjoying the first snowstorm as of yesterday. He mentioned that in only 5 months it will be spring. I think he is optimistic. Living in Alaska makes one resort to almost any kind of lie just to get through another year.

Also in 2002 he sent these two notes:

Nov.
I did send [you an] email about a week ago, but if anything can be done wrong... hear this: I typed in bradengale@hotmale. com. I can see no reason for its not arriving. Can you?

Dec.
You will soon be in our great country! Just a quick suggestion: Bring warm clothing as we will likely spend two or three days in Salt Lake. We would also like to suggest that you bring a fiancée.
More than one would be welcome.
Love, Dad

In 2003 Lindstrom sent his friend, Angelo Garzio, a watercolor painting and photographs. In reply, Garzio wrote:

> *You are one of America's best water colorist[s]. Thank you from the bottom of my heart and soul, for sharing your unique spiritual gift of what the CREATOR has endowed you with. WE, the world, is very much richer for your spiritual vision and it is very moving to look and sense the enthralling emotional reaction a viewer experiences when in front of one [of] these visions. This is what I have tried and unfortunately, have succeeded only rarely in my clay efforts. But when it has come off, oh my!!, what an inexpressible sense it produces. It is as if one sees the presence of GOD and for that brief moment, becomes one with HIM.[130]*

In his last artist's statement, Lindstrom wrote: "I have come to recognize that I am more sensitive now at 85 years, to what I see, and that all seems to contain beauty and is more interesting than ever. I have dozens of ideas I would like to put into visual form."[131] During the last few years of his life, Lindstrom was home-bound and mostly worked on very small paintings, 6 x 8 in. There was a fine historical tradition of such paintings, he said.

"All is well here except for my head," he wrote in an email. "It just doesn't fit right! Tried almost everything except the services of a mechanical engineer." He gave a talk to the docents at the Saint George Art Museum in the gallery that had a number of his paintings on display. The talk, however, "was so bad your mother had to help me out to the car immediately thereafter. I am scheduled to give another talk next Friday at the same place. However, am secretly heading down to Lee's Ferry where there are no communications except by boat."

One evening we went to make some copies of photographs at Kinko's. I had parked along a central street next to the store, alongside a curb. Above the curb was some grass. When we finished photocopying, since I was driving, he walked to the other side of the car to open his door, but it was still locked when he pulled the handle. I was talking to him and then all of a sudden he disappeared. I rushed to the other side of the car; he had fallen on the grass. Water ran down the gutter next to the curb, and he said, while still on his back, "It's nice and cool down here." We laughed. I always marveled at how he could turn something embarrassing into something funny. But that fall would portend other falls, including one at home in which he fractured five ribs.

Late in life, Lindstrom wrote to me: "Just the thought of autumn makes my heart pound. I want to see every leaf that falls. It is an exuberant time for me yet very sad. I miss Logan Canyon so much." Shortly before he died, he emailed:

> *Yesterday I had an extraordinary experience. After spraying some small paintings, we opened the garage door for some fresh air and I thought I would sit on the bench by the front door and then it happened! All in my vision suddenly became brilliantly clear as though an intense white light saturated the entire view: houses, trees, sky, etc. Now I am reluctant to sit there again. I am concerned this "apparition" might not express itself again and also afraid it will.*

Anxious about his health, I called him from the Philippines where I was working. I asked about his interest in so many things. As he aged, he said he "grew more curious." A few weeks later I was on a plane back to Utah to attend Lindstrom's 90th birthday party on July 4th, 2009. Plagued by constant headaches, he always managed to rally when people were in the house. Leslie shot a short video of the artist. In the video he's wearing a single, ill-fitting hearing aid. Although his diminishing appetite shows as he slouches in a chair, belt cinched high above his waist, he's spry and witty, his mind arguably as sharp as when he taught school. He blows out a single candle—"You need 89 more," to which Leslie laughs and replies, "We're broke."

Before I returned to Asia, he asked me to pose with my mother with a flowering oleander as a backdrop while he snapped a half-dozen photographs on his Pentax film camera. "Always take more than one, to ensure you get at least one good one," he taught me. I later retrieved this mother-son photo shoot from the local drugstore's camera department, one of the few places that still developed film. Every photo was blurry. I never showed Lindstrom the photographs. He said a viewer will not forgive you for a photograph without a single plane in focus. In his own photography he prided himself on sharp images, usually with great depth of field.

He still had "much to do," he told my mother a week before he died on August 25, 2009. One of the last paintings he completed, a loose, miniature oil titled *The Old Way*, depicts a Navajo family traveling by horse-drawn cart, the parents' backs to the viewer. He left behind a box marked, "THIS BOX CONTAINS WORK COMPLETED AND MATERIAL FOR NEW PAINTING." Inside were photographs of the Ponte Vecchio bridge, a Butte, Montana house, Aberdeen Harbour boats, and Pine Valley Mountain in southern Utah.

At the graveside service in Salt Lake City, attendees dressed formally in a variety of colors (the artist would have been pleased), a man in paint-splattered jeans coated with sawdust emerged from the nearby woods to watch the service. Afterwards I spoke with him. A former junior high student of Lindstrom's, Layne Nielson said of the artist, "He was a great influence," then he disappeared back into the woods.

There would be one more retrospective, this one at Dixie State University in 2016. In glass cases, like those for the Hitchcock display in Paris, were the artist's cameras and paint brushes surrounded by over 130 works including drawings, paintings, photographs, and ceramics. The show was titled simply "LINDSTROM." Many of the works on display I remembered from childhood. They were arranged chronologically by decade, the 1930s through the 2000s. When my mother first saw the exhibit it moved her to tears. As we strolled the gallery together, we slipped into a living past.

With Lindstrom in retirement and his children grown, Chris and I competed to see who would be the first to visit more countries than our father. I had heard so much about Vietnam growing up and more during the presidential election of 2004, that I had to go. After several days in Hanoi, I traveled to Bac Ha, a small village near the country's border with China. As I wandered the Sunday market overwhelmed by the beauty of the mountains and the Flower Hmong in their traditional dress, I missed my father. As a child I didn't recognize what I came to appreciate as an adult and now greatly miss: The joy of being in the company of my father who loved beauty.

I now live in southern Utah. When I'm alone and driving around the area, although I realize I need to be more careful, I sometimes take my eye off the road, to see what I can see.

Endnotes

1   Ben Fulton, "Artist Brushed Watercolors," *Salt Lake Tribune*, Aug. 27, 2009.
2   Gaell Lindstrom, USU syllabus, Art 101: Exploring Art, Winter Quarter, 1984.
3   Gaell Lindstrom, "Thomas Moran in Utah." 68th Faculty Honor Lecture, Utah State University, Logan, UT, 1984.
4   Gaell Lindstrom, Artist's Statement, 2001.
5   Edith Morgan, "AVA SHOWTIME," *The Herald Journal*, March 25, 1984.
6   Daniel Boorstin, *The Creators* (New York: Random House, 1992), 517.
7   Ibid., 518.
8   "Picasso: Behind Him—and within Him—Lies," LIFE (Dec. 27, 1968): 40.
9   Jean Renoir, *Renoir My Father* (New York: *New York Review of Books*, 2001), 222.
10   Guest Comments: A Tribute to Gaell Lindstrom 1919-2009, St. George, Utah October-January, 2009-10.
11   Gaell Lindstrom, Letter to the Editor, *Salt Lake Tribune*, March 13, 1997.
12   David Ogilvy, *Confessions of an Advertising Man* (London: Southbank, 2012).
13   Gaell Lindstrom, Letter to the Editor, *Salt Lake Tribune*, March 21, 1999.
14   *Renoir My Father*, 116-7.
15   *Vincent van Gogh: Letters from Provence* (New York: Crescent, 1990), 63.
16   Jean Renoir, *Renoir My Father* (New York: New York Review of Books, 2001), 64.
17   Fan Xiaoming, email to Gaell Lindstrom, May 2, 2001.
18   Peter Plagens, "Hopper: The Quiet Man," *Newsweek* (March 2007): 13.
19   Roger Ebert, review of *Dances with Wolves*, directed by Kevin Costner. *Chicago Sun-Times*, November 9, 1990.
20   Matthew Bevis, "It Wants to Go to Bed with Us: John Ashbery's Well-Spent Youth," *Harper's*, June 2017, 92.
21   "One-man Show of Art Set in Cedar City" *Salt Lake Tribune*, Nov. 1952.
22   "Chen Chi: A Great Artist because He's a Great Student," *Outlook* (USU), November, 1971.
23   *Vincent van Gogh: Letters from Provence*, 63.
24   Jeanette Rusk, "Autumn Art: Gaell Lindstrom's Paintings Highlight Seventh Annual Pioneer Courthouse Art Exhibit," *St. George Magazine* (September October 1993).
25   Vern Swanson, Robert Olpin, and William Seifrit, *Utah Art* (Layton, Utah: Gibbs Smith, 1991), 187.
26   Gaell Lindstrom, Interview with Mike Larson.
27   *Renoir My Father*, 266.
28   Gaell Lindstrom Artist's Statement, 2001.
29   *The Creators*, 402.
30   Brett Sokol, "What's it like to be American Art Royalty? Ask the Wyeth Family" *American Way*, July 2017.
31   E. Byrd, "Hold Fast to Wonder!" *The Reader's Digest*.
32   Gaell Lindstrom, "The Cable Mountain Drop," *Ford Times* vol. 52. no. 7 p. 46 (1960, July).
33   *The Creators*, 515.
34   *Renoir My Father*, 357.
35   "Autumn Art: Gaell Lindstrom's Paintings Highlight Seventh Annual Pioneer Courthouse Art Exhibit," *St. George Magazine*.
36   *Vincent van Gogh: Letters from Provence*, 76.
37   "Thomas Moran in Utah"
38   *Renoir My Father*, 223.
39   G. William Richards, letter to Gaell Lindstrom, Sept. 15, 1989.
40   Ibid.
41   Ibid.
42   "His Women: The Wonder is that He Found So Much Time to Paint," Life p. 66.
43   Ibid.
44   *Renior, My Father*, p. 419.
45   Michelle Garrett Bulsiewicz, "Is Utah Upholding Brigham Young's Arts Legacy?" June 21, 2017, *Deseret News*.
46   Annie Adams Kiskadden and Verne Hardin Porter, "The Life Story of Maude," *Green Book Magazine*, June 1914, 892.
47   Brian Maffly, "Lawmaker Laments 'Degrees to Nowhere'." Feb. 4, 2011, *Salt Lake*

    Tribune.

48   Utah Cultural Alliance, "2017 State of Utah Culture."

49   Gaell Lindstrom, *A Brief History of William Gustav Lindstrom*, unpublished.

50   George N. Child, letter to parents, 192.

51   Hugh C. Brown, letter to Lindstrom, January 10, 1938.

52   Clayton Robbins, letter to Lindstrom, July 1999.

53   "Springville Museum of Art", Wikipedia.org.

54   Ruth Harwood, J.T. Harwood Exhibition Program, April 1940.

55   Pat Bagley, "Living History: Original Saltair was a Wonder of the World," July 9, 2012, *Salt Lake Tribune.*

56   Clayton Robbins, letter to Lindstrom, July 1999.

57   Ibid.

58   Salt Lake City Opera Association.

59   Carrie A. Moore, "What's changed at Tabernacle?" March 27, 2007, *Deseret News.*

60   Ibid.

61   Bishop Clarence Tingey, letter to Lindstrom, March 13, 1941.

62   "Rotary Club Hears Slide-Lecture on the Grand Canyon," *Radford News Journal*, June 17, 1943.

63   Graham H. Doxley, letter to Lindstrom, May 25, 1944.

64   John A. Widtsoe, letter to Lindstrom, March 20, 1944.

65   "Elder Brings Relic of Mission Tragedy," *Deseret News* (July 1, 1944).

66   "LeConte Stewart," Utah Artists Project, The University of Utah.

67   Bill Richards, letter to Lindstrom, February 7, 1949.

68   LeConte Stewart and Avard Fairbanks, letter to Lindstrom, June 2, 1949.

69   *Deseret News*, Nov. 27, 1949.

70   Associated Utah Artists, letter to Lindstrom, Nov. 21, 1949.

71   Associated Utah Artists Records, 1940-2006, Archives West.

72   "Lindstrom Work Shown at Art Barn Sunday," *Deseret News* (August 20, 1950).

73   "Summer School at Chester Springs, 1949" brochure, The Pennsylvania Academy of the Fine Arts.

74   "Artists Ride Jeep to the Eastern Session," Newspaper Clipping, Lindstrom papers.

75   Ibid.

76   "Prominent Utahn Works Shown in SL Gallery," Salt Lake Tribune (March 30, 1952).

77   The Church of Jesus Christ of Latter-Day Saints, "House by the Tracks Near River dale."

78   Layne Nielson, interview with Braden Lindstrom, February 22, 2019.

79   LeConte Stewart, letter to Lindstrom, March 19, 1954.

80   "Francis de Erdely," see francisdeerdely.com.

81   Twain Tippetts, letter to Lindstrom, October 26, 1959.

82   George Dibble, "Artist Re-creates Aura of Mine Boom Era," *Salt Lake Tribune*, 1954.

83   Ibid.

84   Dan Valentine, *Salt Lake Tribune* (September 1955).

85   Howard DeVree, "Water-Color Society Includes Works of East," *New York Times* (April 4, 1957).

86   Homer Hacker, "The Founding of the American Watercolor Society," Dec. 5, 1866.

87   John Gutman, "A Career Begins as Another Concludes," *Salt Lake Tribune* (August 12, 1984): E1.

88   Harry Leith-Ross, letter to Lindstrom, March 25, 1957.

89   Nedra Jenkins, "Three New Exhibitions Set for Art Center," *Fort Worth Star Telegram* (Sept. 1957): 14.

90   Beatrice Judd Ryan, letter to Lindstrom, May 7, 1956.

91   Alexander Fried, "Art Annual Presents 'More of the Same," *San Francisco Examiner* (March 27, 1956).

92   Lenore Levers, letter to Lindstrom, December 14, 1957.

93   "USAC Gains Canvas by CSU Artist," *Salt Lake Tribune.*

94   Gaell Lindstrom paper, "The Development of Watercolor Painting," Art History Seminar, California College of Arts and Crafts, July 25, 1962.

95   Edith Morgan, "A Diligent Pursuit of Expressiveness," *The Herald Journal* (April 2, 1990).

96   Twain Tippetts, letter to Lindstrom, May 2, 1957.

97   Ibid.

98   Kathleen Murkock, email, June 24, 2019.

99   Pascal Bonafoux, *Van Gogh: The Passionate Eye,* (London: Thames & Hudson, 1992), 144.

100   Guest Comments: A Tribute to Gaell Lindstrom 1919-2009, St. George, Utah Oct.-Jan. 2009-10.

101   Ibid.

102   Edith Morgan, "AVA—Showtime, *Herald Journal* (March 25, 1984): 22.

103   Andy Watson, interview with Braden Lindstrom, June 9, 2019.

104   *Van Gogh: The Passionate Eye*, 100.

105   Utah State University brochure, 1965.

106   Ibid.

107   Harry Leith-Ross, letter to Lindstrom, July 21, 1963.

108   "Mosaic Mural Dedication Set," *The Herald Journal* (March 3, 1963): 1.

109   "Meanings in the Mosaic Mural," Utah State University brochure, March 1963.

110   "Ten New UMD Faculty Appointments Announced," *Duluth Herald* (August 23, 1973): 17.

111   David London, "Exhibition Review Shimaoka Tatsuzo," Sept. 2001.

112   "Gaell Lindstrom Produces New Indian Portfolio, *Moab Times-Independent* (November 11, 1974).

113   "Utah State University Presents an Exhibit of Paintings and Photographs by Gaell Lindstrom," Utah State University press release, March 1973.

114   Twain Tippetts, letter to Lindstrom, March 16, 1973.

115   George Dibble, "Lindstrom Art Draws Plaudits," *Herald Journal* (March 11, 1973).

116   "Chen Chi: A Great Artist Because He's a Great Student" *Outlook*, Utah State University (November 1971): 6.

117   "Chen-Chi," art-now-and-then.blogspot.com.

118   Diana Kan, *The How and Why of Chinese Painting* (New York: Van Nostrand Reinhold, 1974), 7.

119   Ibid., 8.

120   "Utah State University Presents an Exhibit of Paintings and Photographs by Gaell Lindstrom," Utah State University, March 1973.

121   John Gutman, "A Career Begins as Another Concludes," *Salt Lake Tribune* (August 12, 1984): E1.

122   "Lindstrom Work Goes on Exhibit," *Herald Journal* (March 4, 1973).

123   James Cahill, *Chinese Painting* (New York: Rizzoli International, 1977): 25.

124   The National Gallery of Art, *Catalogue of a Selection of Art Objects from the Freer Collection Exhibited in the New Building of the National Museum* (1912): 26.

125   *The Creators*, 420.

126   John Gutman, "A Career Begins as Another Concludes," *Salt Lake Tribune* (August 12, 1984): E1.

127   George Dibble, "Retrospective Exhibition: GAELL LINDSTROM" program, Nora Eccles Harrison Museum of Art, Utah State University, April 17-June 8, 1986.

128   Ibid., 35.

129   Katherine Kuh, "The Fine Arts," *Saturday Review.* (September 1968): 50.

130   Angelo Garzio, email to Lindstrom, March 28, 2003.

131   Gaell Lindstrom, "Artist's Statement," October 2004.